Crossway Bible Guide

Series editors: Ian Coffey (NT), Stephen Gaukroger (OT)
New Testament editor: Steve Motyer

Titles in this series

Genesis, Richard and Tricia Johnson
Exodus, Stephen Dray
Leviticus, Derek Tidball
Joshua, Charles Price
Ruth and Esther, Debra Reid
Ezra and Nehemiah, Dave Cave
Psalms 1 – 72, Alan Palmer
Psalms 73 – 150, Alan Palmer and Debra Reid
Isaiah, Philip Hacking
Six Minor Prophets, Michael Wilcock
Haggai, Zechariah and Malachi, John James
Matthew's Gospel, Stephen Dray
Mark's Gospel, David Hewitt
Luke's Gospel, Simon Jones
John's Gospel, Ian Barclay
Acts, Stephen Gaukroger
Romans, David Coffey
1 Corinthians, Robin Dowling and Stephen Dray
2 Corinthians, Jonathan Lamb
Ephesians, Steve Motyer
Philippians, Ian Coffey
Colossians and Philemon, Stephen Gaukroger and
    Derek Wood
1 & 2 Thessalonians, Alec Motyer and Steve Motyer
Timothy and Titus, Michael Griffiths
James, David Field
1 Peter, Andrew Whitman
1, 2, 3 John, Diane Tidball

The Bible with Pleasure, Steve Motyer
Discovering the New Testament, Simon Jones
Housegroups: The Leaders' Survival Guide, Ian Coffey and
    Stephen Gaukroger (eds.)
Rebuild, Fran Beckett (ed.)

Ezra and Nehemiah:
Crossway Bible Guide

Dave Cave

Crossway Books Leicester

CROSSWAY BOOKS
38 De Montfort Street, Leicester LE1 7GP, England
Email: ivp@uccf.org.uk
Website: www.ivpbooks.com

This second edition is a revised and edited version of the original book.

First published 1993
Second edition 2003

British Library Cataloguing in Publication Data
A catalogue record for this book is available from the British Library.

ISBN 1–85684–214–2

Set in Palatino
Typeset in Great Britain by Avocet Typeset, Chilton, Aylesbury, Bucks
Printed and bound in Great Britain by Cox & Wyman Ltd,
Reading, Berkshire

CONTENTS

Welcome!

These days, meeting together to study the Bible in groups appears to be a booming leisure-time activity in many parts of the world. In the United Kingdom alone, it is estimated that over one million people each week meet in home Bible-study groups.

This series has been designed to help such groups and, in particular, those who lead them. These Bible Guides are also very suitable for individual study, and may help hard-pressed preachers, teachers and students too (see 'How to use this Bible Guide').

We have therefore enlisted authors who are in the business of teaching the Bible to others and are doing it well. They have kept in their sights two clear aims:

1. To explain and apply the message of the Bible in non-technical language.
2. To encourage discussion, prayer and action on what the Bible teaches.

All of us engaged in the project believe that the Bible is the Word of God – given to us in order that people might discover him and his purposes for our lives. We believe that the sixty-six books which go to make up the Bible, although written by different people, in different places, at different times, through different circumstances, have a single unifying theme: that theme is Salvation. This means free forgiveness and the removal of all our guilt, it means the gift of eternal life, and it means the wholeness of purpose and joy which God has designed us to experience here and now, all of this being made possible through the Lord Jesus Christ.

Five routes through Ezra and Nehemiah

How to use this Bible Guide

These guides have been prepared both for personal study and for the leaders and members of small groups. More information about group study follows on the next few pages.

You can use this book very profitably as a personal study guide. The short studies are ideal for daily reading: the first of the questions provided is usually aimed to help you with personal reflection (see 'How to tackle personal Bible study'). If you prefer to settle down to a longer period of study, you can use groups of three to five studies, and thus get a better overview of a longer Bible passage. In either case, using the Bible Guide will help you to be disciplined about regular study, a habit that countless Christians have found greatly beneficial. (See also 'Five routes through Ezra and Nehemiah' for methods of selecting studies if you do not intend to use them all.)

Yet a third use for these Bible Guides is as a quarry for ideas for the busy Bible teacher, providing outlines and application for those giving talks or sermons or teaching children. You will need more than this book can offer, of course, but the way the Bible text is broken down, comments offered and questions raised may well suggest directions to follow.

How to tackle personal Bible study

We have already suggested that you might use this book as a personal study guide. Now for some more detail.

One of the best methods of Bible study is to read the text through carefully several times, possibly using different versions or translations. Having reflected on the material, it is a good discipline to write down your own thoughts before doing anything else. At this stage it can be useful to consult another background book. See 'Resources' on page 13 and 'For further reading' on page 192. If you are using this book as your main study resource, then read through the relevant sections carefully, turning up the Bible references that are mentioned. The questions at the end of each chapter are specifically designed to help you to apply the passage to your own situation. You may find it helpful to write your answers to the questions in your notes.

It is a good habit to conclude with prayer, bringing before God the things you have learned.

If this kind of in-depth study is too demanding for you and you have only a short time at your disposal, read the Bible passage, read the comments in the Bible Guide, think round one of the questions and commit what you have learned to God in a brief prayer. This would take about fifteen minutes without rushing it.

How to tackle your group Bible study

1. Getting help

If you are new to leading groups, you will obviously want to get all the help you can from ministers and experienced friends. Books are also extremely helpful and we strongly recommend a book prepared by the editors of this series of Bible Guides: *Housegroups: The Leaders' Survival Guide* edited by Ian Coffey and Stephen Gaukroger (Crossway Books, 1996). This book looks at the whole range of different types of group, asking what is the point of it all, what makes a good leader, how to tackle your meeting, how to help the members, how to study, pray, share and worship, and plenty of other pointers, tips and guidelines.

This book is a 'must' for all leaders of small groups. It is written by a team of people widely experienced in this area. It is available at your local Christian bookshop. If you have difficulty in obtaining a copy, write to Crossway Books, Norton Street, Nottingham NG7 3HR, UK.

2. Planning a programme with your Bible Guide

This guide is a commentary on God's Word, written to help group members to get the most out of their studies. Although it is never ideal to chop up Scripture into small pieces, which its authors never intended, huge chunks are indigestible and so we have tried to provide a diet of bite-sized mouthfuls.

If you want to get an overview of the Bible book in a series of meetings, you will need to select appropriate studies for each meeting. Read them yourself first and prepare a short summary of the studies you are tackling for your group. Ideally you could write it on a sheet of A5 paper and hand a copy to each member.

Do not attempt to pack more than one study into one meeting, but choose the crucial one, the study which best crystallizes the message.

If you do not intend to cover the whole Bible book, choose a series of studies to suit the number of meetings you have available. It is a good idea to use consecutive studies, not to dodge about. You will then build up a detailed picture of one section of Scripture. Alternatively, there are five suggested routes through Ezra and Nehemiah on p. 9.

3. Resources

You will find any or all of these books of great value in providing background to your Bible knowledge. Put some of them on your Christmas list and build up your library.

New Bible Dictionary (IVP)
New Bible Atlas (IVP)
New Bible Commentary (21st Century edition) (IVP)
Handbook of Life in Bible Times, John Thompson (IVP)
The Bible User's Manual (IVP)
The Lion Handbook to the Bible (Lion Publishing)
The Message of the Bible (Lion Publishing)
NIV *Study Bible* (Hodder & Stoughton)
The Bible with Pleasure, Steve Motyer (Crossway Books)

The relevant volume in the IVP Tyndale Commentary series will give you reliable and detailed help with any knotty points you may encounter.

4. Preparing to lead

Reading, discussing with friends, studying, praying, reflecting on life … preparation can be endless. But do not be daunted by that. If you wait to become the perfect leader you will never start at all. The really vital elements in preparation are:

▶ prayer (not only in words but an attitude of dependence on God: 'Lord, I can't manage this on my own')

▶ familiarity with the study passage (careful reading of the text, the Bible Guide study and any other resource books that throw light on it) and

▶ a clear idea of where you hope to get in the meeting (notes on your introduction, perhaps, recap what was covered at the last meeting, and what direction you hope the questions will take you in – don't force the group to give your answers).

Here is a short checklist for the busy group leader:

Have I prayed about the meeting?
What do I want to achieve through the meeting?
Have I prepared the material?
Am I clear about the questions that will encourage positive group discussion?
Am I gently encouraging silent members?
Am I, again gently, quietening the chatterers?
Am I willing to admit ignorance?
Am I willing to listen to what the group members say and to value their contributions?
Am I ready not to be dogmatic, not imposing my ideas on the group?
Have I planned how to involve the members in discovering for themselves?

Have I developed several 'prayer points' that will help focus the group?

Are we applying Scripture to our experience of real life or only using it as a peg to hang our opinions on?

Are we finding resources for action and change or just having a nice talk?

Are we all enjoying the experience together?

What can we expect to learn from Ezra and Nehemiah?

Where God intends his people to be
What restoration involves in working together
How leadership should be exercised
How we respond to God's call
How we should maintain God's standards
Lessons from Nehemiah's prayer life
The good news for the poor
How we go about rebuilding our faith

Finding your way around this book

In our Bible Guides we have developed special symbols to make things easier to follow. Every study therefore has an opening section which is the passage in a nutshell.

The main section is the one that makes sense of the passage.

Questions

Every passage also has special questions for personal and group study after the main section. Some questions are addressed to us as individuals, some speak to us as members of our church or home group, while others concern us as members of God's people worldwide. The questions are deliberately designed:

▶ to get people thinking about the passage

▶ to apply the text to 'real life' situations

▶ to encourage reflection, discussion and action!

As a group leader you may well discover additional questions that will have special relevance to your group, so look out for these and note them in your preparation time.

Some passages require an extra amount of explanation, and we have put these sections into two categories.

Digging deeper

The first kind gives additional background material that helps us to understand something factual. For example, if we dig deeper into the Gospels, it helps us to know who the Pharisees were, so that we can see more easily why they related to Jesus in the way they did. These technical sections are marked with a spade.

Stop and think

The second category is marked by a thought-bubble. This feature appears with passages which provide explanations for terms used in the Bible or which highlight important themes or teaching. Bible references and questions are sometimes given as well to help you think through the issues.

Unfolding Ezra and Nehemiah

With the power struggles of the Assyrian, Babylonian and Persian Empires, the Jewish faith had taken a hammering. First the northern kingdom of Israel and then the southern kingdom of Judah had been taken over by the invading armies of the great empires. Many leading families of the tribes of the Hebrew nation had been deported to foreign parts leaving the promised land bereft of effective leadership and the vision, enthusiasm, finance and skills to maintain the holy city of Jerusalem, its temple and the spirituality of the people.

Certain issues were essential to the survival of the people of God.

1. To return to the place where God intended his people to be.
2. To rebuild the temple of God in order to restore his glory.
3. To rebuild the urban priority area of Jerusalem and make it a place where people would want to live.
4. To rebuild the covenant relationship between God and his people through unity of vision, purpose and relationship.
5. To restore and guard the essentials of faith from compromise on a scriptural basis.

Today an increasing proportion of the peoples of the world live in cities so, as in the time of Ezra and Nehemiah, the city is a multinational focus. I believe the call of God is to have faith in the city

The same principals of Ezra/Nehemiah's time apply today.

1. To return to the place where God wants his church to

be. For too long we have observed the decline and departure of the church in the big cities of our land.

2. To rebuild the living temple – the church – as a place of holiness and a place of prayer so that the name of God will no longer be just a curse word on the lips of city-dwellers.

3. To rebuild the urban priority areas – this means Christians getting their hands dirty, dealing with issues ranging from poverty, homelessness, injustice and unemployment to improving the physical environment, thus halting the decline of the presence and impact of the church in the city.

4. To rebuild the faith of Christians living in the city who have lost hope, become apathetic and face conditions which have led to the compromising of the essentials of Christian belief.

5. To restore Christian concern for a biblical basis on which to establish a new morality and vitality which, long term, will affect not only the church but the nation.

The time

It is not always easy to appreciate the context of a story unless it can be viewed in a worldwide setting. The accepted time for Nehemiah's arrival in Jerusalem is 445BC. During 444BC the wall around Jerusalem was completed, but what was happening in the rest of the world?

The Great Pyramid of King Cheops in Egypt was already over 2,000 years old.

The Celtic tribes, also known as Gauls or Galatians, were dominating central and western Europe and Stonehenge was about 800 years old.

Sixty-two years earlier the Etruscan rulers of Italy lost control of the city-state of Rome when their soldiers were routed by Roman soldiers aided by the Greeks.

Thirty-nine years previously an Indian nobleman and religious leader called Buddha died.

Three years earlier work had begun on the Parthenon in Athens.

The place

Five hundred years of kings reigning over the Hebrew nation came to a dramatic end in 587BC when Jerusalem was destroyed and key leaders and people were dragged off into captivity in Babylon.

History shows that the Middle East was a place of power struggles between great empires from Egypt to Iran. For a long time the Assyrian Empire had dominated the lands to the south of the Mediterranean. The Jews had rebelled against its rulers on a number of occasions but the northern kingdom of Samaria finally fell to Sargon II of Assyria in 722BC. Later the Babylonians had beaten the Assyrians and Jerusalem fell to Nebuchadnezzar of Babylon in 597BC, Solomon's temple was destroyed ten years later and mass deportations took place. The Babylonians in turn had succumbed to the Persian nation.

In 538BC the Persian ruler granted permission for all exiles who wished it, to return to their home countries.

The books

Ezra and Nehemiah originally formed one book known as the book of Ezra. The first time they are spoken of as two separate books is by someone in the early church called Origen (AD 185–254). It was not until AD 1448 that the division became completely official as two books in the Hebrew bible.

1. Who wrote the books and when?

The suggestion is that the author is the same person who wrote Chronicles. That is because the final verses of 2 Chronicles are almost identical to Ezra 1:1–3. Certainly there is a lot of common ground between Chronicles and Ezra/Nehemiah.

For example, both show a great deal of interest in sacred vessels of the temple (1 Chronicles 28:13–19; 2 Chronicles 5:1; and Ezra 1:7; 7:19; 8:25–30, 33–34).

Also, the order of sacrifices and sacrificial materials is

almost identical (2 Chronicles 2:3; 8:13 and Ezra 3:4–6; and 1 Chronicles 29:21; 2 Chronicles 29:21, 32 and Ezra 6:9, 17; 7:17–18, 22; 8:35–36). Liturgical music and instruments, as well as those who are involved, are very much the same (1 Chronicles 15:19; 16:5–6; 25:1, 6; 2 Chronicles 5:12–13 and Ezra 3:10; Nehemiah 12:35).

The major theme of Chronicles is renewal and reform based on a return to religious faithfulness after years of impurity. The pattern of Ezra/Nehemiah is very similar.

Some say the author is Ezra the scribe. If it is Ezra, we know he arrived back in Jerusalem in 458BC and so he must have written it sometime later. It is reasonable to suggest that on this basis it was completed by 400BC. Whoever wrote it, one thing is clear, they drew upon a number of sources.

2. Sources for both books are based partly on personal diaries

Ezra's diary includes the letter to Artaxerxes (Ezra 7:12–26), Ezra's caravan (Ezra 8:1–14) and the section on mixing with foreigners (Ezra 10:18–43).

Nehemiah's diary records the building of the wall (Nehemiah 3) and the home-comers (Nehemiah 7:6–73).

3. Letters in Ezra are written in Aramaic

Parts of Ezra are written in Aramaic, the official language of Persian diplomats, rather than Hebrew, the language of the Jews. These sections include a number of official letters: one to Ahasuerus (4:7) and another to Artaxerxes (4:8), a letter to Darius (5:7–17) and Darius's reply (6:2–12) and a copy of a letter by Cyrus (6:25).

4. Registers of names

It is obvious that both Ezra and Nehemiah had access to records, most long since lost, which include registers of signatories, names and places (Ezra 2:2–61; 8:2–20; 10:18–43; Nehemiah 3:1–31; 7:7–63; 10:1–27; 11:4–36; 12:1–26, 32–35, 41–42).

5. Date of Ezra and Nehemiah

Various suggestions for the dating of Ezra and Nehemiah have been made, but one thing which is certain is that they could not have been written before 430BC because of the events which are recorded. Ezra is active in 458BC, and Nehemiah returned to Jerusalem in 445BC.

Some scholars have argued for a date of around 300BC because they identify Jaddua (Nehemiah 12:10–11) as the one mentioned by Josephus as living during the time of Alexander the Great. This is unlikely (see p. 169).

A more popular view in recent times is to date Ezra and Nehemiah at around 400BC because there is no hint of the Greek invasions of Alexander the Great in the text, nor the rebellion against King Artaxerxes by the Jews and the Phoenicians during the middle of the fourth century BC.

So I would suggest Ezra and Nehemiah were written somewhere between 430 and 400BC.

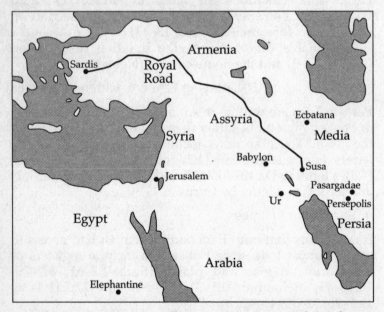

The Persian Empire at the time of Ezra and Nehemiah

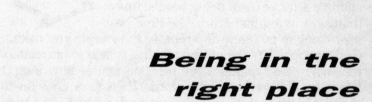

Being in the right place

Ezra 1:1 – 2:7

Ezra 1:1–4

God rules OK!

God is in control of his creation and he is God of all the nations not just Israel. He always keeps his promises and not only is his authority unlimited but he can and does speak even to unbelievers.

Here begins the powerful story of a group of people returning to their home country after years of being held against their will in another land. The time has now come to go home and rebuild the temple and restore God's people. Ezra begins by making it clear to his readers that when God makes a promise, no matter how long it takes, he always keeps his word. Then Ezra goes on to make it plain that it is God's Spirit who stirs King Cyrus of the Persians into action.

'The word of the LORD spoken by Jeremiah' (verse 1) refers to the prophecies in Jeremiah 25:11 and 29:10 which promise that the people will be set free after seventy years. Some think that a week is a long time; seventy years must have seemed an eternity to those waiting on the fulfilment of God's promise through Jeremiah.

Even more significantly, when Cyrus carried out God's promise and gave the Jews permission to go home, the majority did not want to. For years they had prayed for deliverance from captivity and complained that they could not praise God in a foreign land (Psalm 137), but many had done well in business and now a conflict arose between material comforts and spiritual direction. Only the tribes of Judah and Benjamin, plus an assortment of priests and Levites, responded to God's call to go home in order to restore the temple, the city and the nation.

Judah, mentioned in verse three, was the southern half of the land of Israel which split from the north after the death of Solomon (1 Kings 12:20) and included the city of Jerusalem. The two main tribes occupying this area of Israel were Judah, part of Benjamin which was incorporated into Judah (the other part joining the northern kingdom), and Simeon. It was viewed by biblical writers as the more godly of the two kingdoms because it remained loyal to the house of David, God's chosen king. As the majority of those who returned from Babylon came from Judah, the word Jew now came into common use to describe those who came from Israel.

The freewill offering (verse 6) would be an offering made specifically for the rebuilding of the temple rather than for provisions for the people who were setting off back to Israel. Perhaps it eased the consciences of those who had chosen to stay behind when they put their hands in their pockets to help those who were actually going to do the work.

It was time to go home; the waiting was over and faith was rewarded. Empires may come and go, but God keeps his promises to all who put their trust in him. The words of Isaiah take on a new freshness, 'Even youths grow tired and weary, and young men stumble and fall; but those who hope in the LORD will renew their strength' (Isaiah 40:30–31).

The Jews waited nearly two thousand years after the fall of Jerusalem to the Romans to see the nation of Israel re-established in 1948. How many times they must have questioned Old Testament promises assuring them that God would never forget his people. They endured persecution over the centuries from the crusaders from Europe to the Tsars of Russia, from Hitler's holocaust to Arabs. They suffered the bigotry of literature from Shakespeare's Shylock to Charles Dickens' Fagan, but there was always a faithful remnant of the covenant people who were never shaken from the conviction that God is in control and working his purposes out. The message is consistent from the beginning of Ezra to the end of Nehemiah, and is still

the same today – God is King of kings and Lord of lords.
God rules OK!

Questions

1. Patience is listed as one of the fruit of the Spirit
   (Galatians 5:22). How would you cope if God told you
   to wait seventy years before he answered your prayers?
2. Which do you think is easiest – to do what God asks you
   to do, or pay for someone else to do it for you?
3. How does the church explain to others that God is in
   control when, in the short term, evil seems to triumph?

Biblical terms

The God of heaven (verse 2)
This is a title used in the Persian period to refer to the God
of Israel. Before this time it was one of the titles of the
Canaanite god of storms, Baal-Hadad. It was not uncom-
mon for a nation to apply titles to their god formerly given
to the gods of nations they had defeated in battle.

It was used regularly by Jews speaking to foreigners
about their God and occurs in this context a number of
times in Ezra and Nehemiah (Ezra 1:2; 5:11–12; 6:9–10;
7:12, 21, 23; Nehemiah 1:4–5; 2:4, 20). It is used frequently
in the *Elephantine Papyri* (the name given to a number of
texts dating from the fifth century discovered in AD 1906 at
Elephantine Island on the river Nile in Egypt regarding
life in a Jewish colony there).

King Cyrus would also have recognized it as a title of
the Zoroastrian god Ahura Mazda. It was believed he
alone was god and created man, darkness and the light
(hence the lightbulb of that name).

Ezra 1:5–11

Moved by God

It is important to be both spiritually inspired and practically equipped for God's work.

Sheshbazzar, made governor of Judah by Cyrus, led the return, restoring the people to the land. He also laid the temple foundations and returned the temple vessels to Jerusalem. Ezra would return later to complete the restoration of the temple.

'Everyone whose heart God had moved' (verse 5) prepared themselves for the task ahead. Money, valuables and livestock were as important as hearts full of enthusiasm for God's call and commission. He had moved the heart of the Persian king, so he could move anybody. Now the enthusiasm was infectious and everyone was getting involved. The whole people of God have a responsibility and a part to play in assisting the work of the kingdom to progress and at that time virtually every Jew in Babylon was involved: giving to the cause, or helping members of the family who were going back to Jerusalem prepare for the journey.

In the New Testament Cleopas and his friend described how their hearts burned when the resurrected Jesus spoke and shared scriptures with them. But it was only in the practical action of breaking bread that they recognized Jesus for who he was (Luke 24:30–32).

When people are moved by God it may begin with the heart but must also include time, talents and treasures. Unlike a game of football where twenty-two people put their time and energy into the game while thousands sit and stand around the pitch shouting advice, all who are on the Lord's side have a part to play practically as well as spiritually. Real spirituality is always practical when we are moved by God.

Questions

1. How do you react when someone offers you advice on a particular situation when it is obvious that they have no intention of doing anything practical to help?
2. Many well-known Christians have described how a great work of God began in their lives when their hearts were affected. Have you ever felt like that?
3. Paul wrote that God would supply all your needs (Philippians 4:19). How does he do that in your church?

Background

The inventory (verses 9–10)
These vessels are not specifically named. What kinds of vessels they were can be discovered by reading 2 Kings 24:14–15. The gold and silver dishes or basins were probably used for pouring out wine (or blood) offerings to God. The number of articles is probably taken from a temple receipt. Verse 11 mentions 5,400 vessels, the number of items in the Hebrew text is 2,499 but that is probably only a list of the more significant vessels on the inventory. Now they would all be returned to their rightful home in the temple in Jerusalem under the watchful eye of Sheshbazzar.

Know who you are and where your roots are.

Ezra 2, with some slight variations, appears as Nehemiah 7:6–73. The province mentioned in verse 1 is Judah and not Babylon. It is a sort of *who's who* of those who returned from exile and later generations would look back at it with great pride if their families and villages were mentioned. Over 50% of the list of names are those of families (verses 2–20) and nearly 30% are names of villages (verses 21–35). The rest of the record is made up of priests (verses 36–39), Levites, singers, gatekeepers and temple servants (verses 40–58).

Away from home, roots become much more important and, in very much the same tradition as I grew up with in North Wales, people are described by either their families or the places they came from. For the Jews, as well as the Irish, the Welsh and the Scots, knowing where they have come from can be nearly as important as where they are going to. After all, only the descendant of a priest could become a priest – it was very much a father and son business. You had to be able to prove your mother was Jewish in order to establish yourself as Jewish. Hence the dilemma of those listed in verse 59 and following.

In any historic list of names there will always be one family name which looms larger and appears more significant than the rest. This one is no exception, and the name Parosh is the largest family listed. Others of the same family are recorded as having returned with Ezra (8:3) and more bearing the same name are among those who helped Nehemiah rebuild the walls of Jerusalem (Nehemiah

3:25). Interestingly the name means 'Flea', and the implication may be that although small, it is capable of making its mark on something or someone much larger than itself. David, in a conversation with Saul, implied that he, David, was regarded as a flea (1 Samuel 24:14; 26:20). The name probably had more significance then than is now apparent.

Zerubbabel (verse 2) probably means 'Seed of Babylon' or 'Born in Babylon'. This man was the grandson of Jehoiachin (Ezra 3:2; Haggai 1:1; Matthew 1:12). He returned with the second group, after Sheshbazzar, in 520BC in order to rebuild the temple and is normally associated with Jeshua. Accounts found in the books of Haggai and Zechariah show how he was thought by some, for a while, to be messiah – especially as he was a descendant of David (1 Chronicles 3:19). But Ezra does not seem to share that view as he makes no mention of it.

Jeshua (verse 2) is an Aramaic version of Joshua. He was descended from the last chief priest, Jozadak (1 Chronicles 5:41), and was probably made high priest at Jerusalem as a result (Zechariah 3:1). Incidentally, in Aramaic the name for Jeshua is Jesus, and Jesus would have been known as Jeshua by his family.

Questions

1. Where did your family live three generations ago?
2. Do you think there should be ethnic churches – Welsh, Irish or African, for example? Or should there be one international church for everybody?
3. How would you demonstrate your relationship to Jesus?

Biblical terms

The captivity (verse 1)

This is normally used as a technical term to describe the period of time that the tribes of Israel were forcibly restrained from going back home.

In 722BC the northern kingdom of Israel was overrun by the Assyrian army and its king Sargon II, and all but the poor were taken away from their homeland and resettled in Mesopotamia (2 Kings 17:6). Later, under a new king, Sennacherib, the Assyrians captured 66 cities from the southern kingdom of Judah in 701BC.

Then in 598BC, after the Babylonians had defeated the Assyrians and taken over their empire, Jerusalem was captured and most of its leading citizens also taken to Babylon. By 586BC the southern kingdom was finished and the temple destroyed (2 Kings 25:12).

Not much is known about what happened to the exiles in the sixty years after the fall of Jerusalem, except that King Jehoiachin was released when Evil-Merodach became king of Babylon in 561BC (2 Kings 25:27–30) and is mentioned in Babylonian records.[1]

Finally, in 538BC after the Persians had defeated the Babylonians, King Cyrus gave permission for the Jews to return home to their own land, but only a few would return. The rest stayed to become part of what would be known as the *Diaspora* (the Jews of the dispersion).

Personnel

Priests (verse 36)

Priests in Israel were the descendants of Aaron, Moses' brother (Numbers 10:8). Unlike priesthood in the church, it was not a vocation but an office: kings were called or chosen by God but not priests. The word which is

31

translated 'appoint' or 'consecrate' (e.g. Exodus 28:41) refers to the making of priests, and means literally 'to fill the hand' and probably originates in the fact that Moses put parts of sacrifices into the hands of Aaron and his sons (Exodus 29:24–25; Leviticus 8:27–28).

Priests were not ordained as such, but they were set apart for God's service and so could set foot on holy ground and handle sacred objects without causing them to become unclean. In order to carry out these tasks, priest were forbidden to do certain things. For instance, they could not attend funerals, except for those of close family (Leviticus 21:1–6). Priests were not allowed to marry prostitutes or divorcees (Leviticus 21:7) and had to put on special clothes to enter God's sanctuary, as well as wash their clothes (Exodus 28:43) and abstain from alcohol (Leviticus 10:8–11).

Ezra 2:40–58

The house of the Lord

Every one of God's people has a part to play in the house of the Lord.

The 'big name' families came first, as is often the case, then the priests. The list continues now with the names of the families of Levites, singers, gatekeepers and temple servants. In an ever constant concern to cover every detail, a note is made of every single task necessary to ensure the house of the Lord could function effectively. It would take all the families and their particular skills to allow the temple to function as God intended, unless they were unable to show they were truly God's people.

In times past, during the monarchy, the temple had fallen into disrepair on a number of occasions because not everyone had carried out their responsibilities. King Joash had to repair the temple (2 Chronicles 24:4) and King Hezekiah actually had to have the doors re-opened and order the Levites to clean out the temple: a bit like a child who has not cleaned his room for a long time (2 Chronicles 29:3–36). In the time of King Josiah, when he was eighteen years old, it was again necessary to purify the house of the Lord (2 Chronicles 34:8). This time things had grown so out of hand that the temple staff had managed to lose the Book of the Law, God's written word, and it was only rediscovered during the spring-cleaning (2 Chronicles 34:14).

With this backcloth you can appreciate why it was important to ensure everything was done decently and in order. Church premises today suffer the same problems; shabby buildings and surroundings because Christians have opted out of their responsibilities. The issue also arises in the temple (the gathered congregation of Christians) when believers do not give attention to their duties and responsibilities. The apostle Paul wrote to admonish the church at Corinth because they were gossiping, arguing with each other, taking one another to court and there was even sexual immorality. He said, 'Don't you know that you yourselves are God's temple and that God's Spirit lives in you?' (1 Corinthians 3:16).

Every believer is a part of the house of the Lord, with a duty and responsibility to play his or her part properly.

Questions

1. Do you recognize the responsibilities God has placed on you personally?
2. What are the areas of need in the church you attend in order to maintain an effective Christian witness?
3. In the worldwide church would you say God's house is in order?

Personnel

Levites (verse 40)

The sons of Levi were set apart in order to perform certain sacred functions, such as looking after the tabernacle or tent of meeting during the exodus (Numbers 1:50). They had the responsibility of helping Aaron and his descendants in their priestly role (1 Chronicles 6:48–49). They did not inherit land as the other tribes did (Deuteronomy 10:8–9) but they were provided with an income and allocated towns amongst the other tribes in which to live (Numbers 35:1–8).

One clan within the tribe of Levi was promised inherited priesthood, Aaron's family (Exodus 29:9, 44; 40:15; Numbers 3:4), while the rest of the tribe performed the less important functions. Although it must be said that during the time of Judges and up to the time of David not all priests were from the tribe of Levi (Judges 17:5; 1 Samuel 1:1; 2 Samuel 20:6). Jeroboam I also made non-Levitical priests but was not approved of for having done so (1 Kings 12:31–32). But even at this time it was considered preferable to have a priest from the tribe of Levi.

The fact that Levites were considered less important than priests may have had something to do with the reluctance of many of them to return to Israel after the exile (Ezra 8:15–29).

If you are not sure where you fit in – find out.

Everybody wants to feel that they are accepted and belong. Those families which Ezra lists in verse 59 would be no exception. They could not be involved in the temple and share in the portion of food for the priests (Leviticus 2:3) unless they could provide the missing links in their family trees.

Three priestly families and three non-priestly families could not prove they were of good Jewish stock. It may have been that they had lost their family records, although it seems unusual that no-one would remember at least some of their ancestors, especially as genealogies were considered important. What was more likely was that they had intermarried in Babylon with people from other nations. This could make it impossible to show an un-broken line of Jewish descent. As a result, they were regarded as unclean. This meant that those from the priestly families were not allowed to function as such. They were not permitted to eat the sacred food until the will of God had been sought by the use of Urim and Thummim. The order came straight from the top, from the governor himself (verse 63). It was a strong incentive to find the missing links in order to fit into the family and the purposes of God. God would have the final say.

Jesus' family tree (set out in Matthew 1) would have raised one or two eyebrows at the time of Ezra. Four women are mentioned in it and three of the four were not of Jewish origin! Rahab (verse 5) was a Canaanite and ran the local bordello in Jericho (Joshua 2:1). Ruth, David's grandmother (verse 5), was a Moabite (Ruth 1:4). Uriah's wife, Bathsheba (verse 6) was a Hittite, or at least married to one (2 Samuel 11:3).

Most church traditions today operate a system of safeguards for sharing bread and wine. It normally requires some rite acknowledging membership of the family of God: membership, baptism or confirmation. Some churches will allow only members of their own particular denomination to participate.

The missing link for those outside the church today is Jesus Christ. He is the only one who can bring us back into a right relationship with the heavenly Father. The challenge is still the same today: if you are not sure where you fit in, find out.

Questions

1. What do you think is the minimum requirement needed to be called a Christian?
2. What proof should Christians look for in order to relate to other Christians?
3. Who should decide who is acceptable and who is not in the church?

Temple worship

Urim and Thummim (verse 63)

No-one knows for certain exactly what they were or what the words actually mean. From Bible references, however, we know that they were kept in the breastplate, or ephod, of the garments of the high priest (Exodus 28:6–30) and were used to discern God's will in times of uncertainty (Numbers 27:21; 1 Samuel 14:41–42; 23:9–12).

Three answers could be achieved by consulting Urim and Thummim, also known as the sacred lots: yes, no, or neither (a bit like heads and tails in the tossing of coins). They were entrusted to the tribe of Levi (Deuteronomy 33:8). After the time of King David there is little evidence that they were used and people took to asking prophets or seers to discern the will of God for them. The only other mentions are in this verse and Nehemiah 7:65 which suggests there was no priest who could use them. Nehemiah 10:34 mentions the 'casting of lots' by the priests.

Ezra 2:64–70

Everything but the kitchen sink!

It is important in responding to God's call not to forget the practical requirements.

These few verses include quite an inventory of people and property. The total of 42,360 (verse 64) is a lot more than those who are actually mentioned. If you add the men of Israel (24,144), the priests (4,289), the Levites, singers and servants (733) and those of unknown families (652), the total comes to 29,818. The gap is probably bridged by adding on women and children who are not mentioned.

Horses, mules, camels and donkeys are on the list, too, but not sheep, goats and cattle. It has been argued that they were not a part of this great caravan because they would have slowed it down significantly.

It seems that everything which was vital for the task was included: the various ministries from priests to musicians; lay people, servants and slaves; horses for military work, mules for the powerful and wealthy, camels to transport heavy loads and donkeys to carry women, children and other loads. Everything, in fact, except the kitchen sink!

Finance was also a practical consideration, if the temple was to be rebuilt. It was not raised by jumble sales, street-by-street collection, or appeals. It was direct giving by the leaders of the families in the form of a freewill offering. The total amount was pretty substantial. One drachma, if it was a Persian daric, was equivalent to one month's wages for a soldier. They could have argued that the money was needed for them to resettle in and around Jerusalem (verse 70), but they didn't. Real giving, sacrificial giving, came from the conviction that the Lord had need of it. This was a practical demonstration of their faith as well as a witness to the surrounding nations. When they arrived in Jerusalem the people proved their conviction by their giving (verse 68).

An old hymn reflects the kitchen-sink approach: 'Take my life and let it be consecrated, Lord, to thee ... take my silver and my gold, not a mite would I withhold.' Each verse builds up the inventory and the message comes over clearly: *'Use me and everything I have – including the kitchen sink!'*

Questions

1. What method do you use in deciding what to give to God's work?
2. How does your church raise money to carry out the work of the kingdom of God?
3. Is there anything you would not give up for God?

Restoring the
temple

Ezra 3:1 – 6:22

Ezra 3:1–7

Tabernacles and trumpets

The priority of God's people is to give him first place.

The first return was complete, now it was time to re-establish temple worship in Jerusalem. In the seventh month (equivalent to our September/October) the people gathered 'as one man' (verse 1), a phrase which would not be used again until Nehemiah 8.

The ritual sacrifice of an animal (or sometimes a person) to a particular deity was common among the nations in Old Testament times. Leviticus 1:3–17, which covers the requirements of burnt offerings, suggests they were made to obtain forgiveness or atonement (Leviticus 1:4) and that the result is a pleasing smell to God (Leviticus 1:9, 13, 17).

The Feast of Tabernacles (verse 4) was usually celebrated on the fifteenth day of the month of Tishri (Exodus 23:16; 34:22). It lasted a week and marked the end of the gathering in of grapes. In order to gather in the harvest, many folk went out in the fields and lived in tents, and so the occasion was used as a reminder of the time of Moses when the Jewish people lived in tents for forty years. The word 'tabernacle' means 'tent of meeting' and was used of the mobile place of worship where the ark of the covenant was kept during the wilderness period of the nation's history; it can also mean 'temporary shelters'.

The foundation of the temple had yet to be laid (verse 6), but that did not stop the Israelites from celebrating in times of worship and sacrifice in complete unity.

It is all too easy to find reasons (excuses?) for not giving God first place. In the New Testament we read of people who came to follow Jesus, but had a variety of excuses for putting off a response (Luke 9:57–62). I wonder what would have happened if the believers gathered in the Upper Room at Pentecost (Acts 1) had decided to get everything right before they went out to proclaim the good news? They would first have had to find a building to meet in, raised the money for the mission, decided on an agreed theology, and waited for a well-qualified leader – but they didn't. God was given first place and everything else followed. Jesus simply said 'Seek first his kingdom and his righteousness, and all these things will be given to you as well' (Matthew 6:33).

Whatever the cost, nothing is achieved by putting off doing God's will; the priority of God's people is always to give him first place.

Questions

1. What excuses have you used for putting off God's will in your life?
2. If you wait for everything to be perfect before you do anything, how long will you have to wait?
3. Is there such a thing as the perfect church on earth?

Geography

Sidon (verse 7)
Sidon was a Phoenician port on the coast of Lebanon and a centre of commerce and industry at the time of Ezra.

Tyre (verse 7)
The city of Tyre was the main port of the Phoenicians and was about 40 kms south of Sidon. It had two harbours, one on the mainland and one on an island opposite.

The people of Tyre were well known as traders and merchants, as well as slave-traders (Joel 3:5–6). Jesus

41

visited the area near to Tyre (Matthew 15:21–28), and the people of Tyre listened to him speak (Mark 3:8 and Luke 6:17).

Lebanon (verse 7)
Lebanon was a mountain range in Syria famous for its trade in timber. The southern end was a continuation of the hills of Galilee. 160 kms long, it was covered with thick forests of myrtles, conifers and cedars. It is often described in the Old Testament as a place of plenty (e.g. Psalm 72:16; Hosea 14:5–7).

The cedars of Lebanon were seen as symbols of power and might (Judges 9:15; 1 Kings 4:33; 2 Kings 14:9; Isaiah 35:2; 60:13) and were used for the great temples and palaces of the surrounding nations, including Israel (1 Kings 5:6, 9 and 14).

Joppa (verse 7)
Joppa is the old name for the present-day port of Jaffa which extends to Tel Aviv in Israel. It was the nearest natural harbour to Jerusalem, some 55 kms inland, and so was the obvious place to ship materials to for the building of the temple. It was from this port that Jonah set sail in a ship to escape God's will for him (Jonah 1:3) and Peter stayed at Simon the tanner's house in Joppa (Acts 10:32).

Ezra 3:8–13

A firm foundation

Make sure the foundation for your faith is right.

The second month of the Jewish calendar is equivalent to our April/May. It is interesting to note that Zerubbabel and Jeshua chose this particular time to lay the temple foundation. Solomon chose the same time to carry out the same task with the first temple (1 Kings 6:1)

The required age for anyone serving as a Levite had originally been thirty years and over (Numbers 8:24), but at this time it was lowered to twenty (verse 8). The age seems to have been reduced at the time of the building of Solomon's temple also (1 Chronicles. 23:24–27), so it appears that they were following the same pattern as Solomon in order to ensure the foundations were properly laid.

The physical task of laying the foundations was followed by a time of celebration, 'as prescribed by David' (verse 11), which included thanksgiving and praise (verse 12). The word used here for joy (verses 12 and 13, and in Ezra 6:16, 22; Nehemiah 8:10, 12, 17; 12:43), suggests a smiling face and means 'excitement' or 'gladness'. It is not just applied to an individual but to the community as well. It is seen as a quality as well as an emotion, and is frequently linked to the national and religious life experiences of Israel (Nehemiah 8:10–11). In the Old Testament it was a mark of the Golden Age (Isaiah 49:13) and in the New Testament it is listed as one of the main fruits of the Holy Spirit (Galatians 5:22).

A firm foundation was laid because they had followed the instructions set out in God's Word; they laid a firm foundation not only for the building but also in their hearts. They had laid a foundation for their faith in obeying God's instructions.

Later, as we shall see, they began to compromise and water-down God's Word for them and things changed as a result, but at least the temple would be built on a firm foundation.

Questions

1. Do you ever take short-cuts in the Christian life? If so, what is usually the result?
2. What do you think happens when a church ignores God's instructions?
3. How can you build a firm foundation for your faith?

Temple worship

Vestments (verse 10)

During religious celebrations the priests would wear vestments, normally a linen garment worn around the waist. Sometimes called a linen ephod (1 Samuel 2:18), it was probably a loin-cloth or apron.

The high priest wore a tunic of blue. Over it he wore the robe of the ephod decorated with pomegranates and bells and over this he wore an ephod made of gold. Finally over all the vestments he wore the embroidered breastplate. This was the jewel-covered pouch carrying the sacred lots Urim and Thummim. He also wore a white cloak and a special turban (see Exodus 28).

Bribery and corruption

Whenever God calls people to carry out his work, the enemy will always be there to try and undermine God's authority.

 As soon as work on the temple began in earnest, the enemies of those who had returned moved in. They devised an interesting strategy to foil the efforts of Israel in rebuilding the temple.

They began with an attempt at infiltration: 'Let us help you build' (verse 2), with an appeal to common ground for faith. At first it seems a reasonable request, until you understand the background.

After the fall of Samaria, the Assyrian invaders followed a familiar pattern of the times by taking away the leading families and replacing them with similar people from other nations. Consequently, the former northern kingdom of Israel developed a kind of mixed faith that was no longer regarded as pure. However, when the Babylonians took leading families into exile from Judah, Benjamin and Jerusalem they did not replace them. This meant the former southern kingdom remained loyal to Yahweh (the name for God).

Following the model of a right foundation, there could be no compromise. 'Cleanliness is next to godliness' took on a much stronger implication here. The rebuke by Zerubbabel, Jeshua and the leaders is carefully worded: 'You have no part ... we alone will build it for the LORD (Yahweh), the God of Israel, as king Cyrus ... commanded us' (verse 3). They named the authority of the king and God in dismissing their enemies, appealing to both civil and religious authority.

'The peoples around them' (verse 4), or more literally 'the people of the land' and interchangeable with 'peoples' used already in Ezra 3:3, refers to the inhabitants of Judah, Samaria, Idumea and other neighbouring regions who are not authentic Jews and therefore religiously suspect (see also Ezra 9:1–2, 11; 10:2, 11; Nehemiah 9:24, 30; 10:31–32).

Having failed to water things down from the inside, the people around them set about attempting to discourage them from the outside. The word 'discourage' (verse 4) in Hebrew literally means 'to weaken the hands', so they would not be able to carry out the work (compare 6:22 and Nehemiah 6:4). Fear is often a good weapon: it had worked very well for Gideon's three hundred against thousands (Judges 7:16–25); now Israel's enemies were trying the same technique against them, but to little effect.

Finally, the opposition hired counsellors to try and intimidate the Jews: a similar method to that used later to intimidate Nehemiah (Nehemiah 13:2).

Corruption and bribery failed because Israel was convinced that not only the king, but the King of kings was on their side. I wonder if Paul had a situation like this in mind when he wrote in Romans 8:31, 'if God is for us, who can be against us?'

Questions

1. If a Jehovah's Witness or a Mormon asked to help in your church, what would you do?
2. What makes you afraid and how do you deal with that fear?
3. How can we demonstrate God's authority as Christians?

Take a letter!

There have always been those who are ready to spread scandal about God's people in order to try and destroy their credibility.

Someone once said 'the pen is mightier than the sword', now Israel's enemies were out to prove it. They wrote a letter to the authorities accusing the Jews of rebellion, claiming they were restoring Jerusalem in order to plot against the king. The word used for 'accusation' (Sitna) is close to the word 'Satan'.

Aramaic (verse 7) at this period was the common language of the Persian Empire (all of Ezra 4:8 – 6:18 is written in Aramaic, as is Ezra 7:12–26). It is quite close to Hebrew in structure and was originally the language of another semitic people, the Aramaeans. Jacob (Deuteronomy 26:5) referred to himself as an Aramaean, which suggests quite close links. Aram is the biblical name for Syria.

The Persian king made use of many people across the empire to keep him informed of any possible threat to his authority. In Jerusalem it appears his informers were Bishlan, Mithsedath, Tabeel (verse 7), Rehum and Shinshai (verse 8), and it was these men who wrote the accusing letter. They include themselves in the numbers of deportees living in and around Samaria and the Trans-Euphraates.

Then they applied another favourite strategy of the dissatisfied. If the rebuilding were to be allowed, 'no more taxes, tribute or duty will be paid and the royal revenues will suffer' (verse 13). Not only were they trying to undermine Israel, now they were directly challenging the authority of the king. A similar situation is still common today: big businesses who don't like Christian influence on the law of the land attack government where it feels most pain: in its purse!

Tax was a fixed annual tribute paid by the province. Tribute was a kind of poll tax, and duty was due to a feudal lord (it could be called protection money) and accounted for much individual taxation. All together it has been estimated that Persia took from the Jews, Samaritans and Gentiles of Palestine something in the region of 350 silver talents.[2] A talent was equivalent to about 300 people's wages for one year!

It was the king's turn to send a letter. A search had been made in the library and some history of revolt had been recorded (see 2 Kings 18:7; 24:1) and so the order was given for work on the temple to cease (verse 23). The Jews were forced to stop work and they had no choice but to obey. Scandal had undermined credibility in the short term, but not for too long: 'until the second year of the reign of Darius, King of Persia' (verse 24).

The second year of the reign of King Darius began on 1 Nissan 520BC (estimated as 3 April), with work on the temple beginning on 21 September, according to J. Finegan.[3] When the work was stopped, the Persian Empire was under threat from a variety of rebels, and only once things were stable would the task of rebuilding be permitted to continue, but it would continue.

The history of the church follows a similar pattern. The people carrying out God's work have been persistently scandalized: John Wesley, for example, was maligned, often being stoned and beaten up for preaching the Good News, but he persevered in proclaiming God's kingdom. The early founders of the Pentecostal movement just after the turn of the twentieth century, were treated in the same way, but through persistence have established their credibility in the Christian world.

The church has been maligned, persecuted and prevented from carrying out its work by empires from Rome to Russia, but still the words of Jesus ring true: 'On this rock I will build my church, and the gates of Hades will not overcome it' (Matthew 16:18).

Questions

1. What sort of pressure has been used to stop you going to church?
2. How is money used against the church today?
3. Why does the press usually focus on stories which are about scandal amongst Christians?

Geography

Samaria and the Trans-Euphrates (verse 10)
Samaria (verse 10) was the capital city of the northern kingdom of Israel from the time of King Omri (1 Kings 16:24). When it was destroyed by the Assyrians in 721BC, around 27,000 of its leading citizens were taken off into captivity in Assyria (2 Kings 17:24) and replaced by captives from other nations. The newcomers, together with one of the Jewish priests in exile, set up a place of worship at Bethel and a sort of mixed faith developed, partly based of the God of Israel and partly on the gods of the foreigners now inhabiting Samaria (2 Kings 17:25–34). This was why the Jews returning from exile refused to allow them to have anything to do with the rebuilding of the temple. They were now regarded as impure. Later, some of the Samaritans would set up their own place of worship at Shechem, centred on Mount Gerezim (Deuteronomy 11:29; Joshua 8:33), which led to the question put to Jesus by the Samaritan woman (John 4:19–20).

Trans-Euphrates (verse 10), or 'the province beyond the river' are the words used in Hebrew, and refer to the Persian province west of the Euphrates river, which included Palestine and Syria. It is often referred to simply as 'the river' (Deuteronomy 11:24) in the Old Testament.

Personalities

Xerxes (verse 6)
Also known in Hebrew as Ahasuerus, he was one of the Persian rulers. The beginning of his reign (verse 6) refers to the point when he came to power and not when he came to the throne (486–465BC).Verses 6–23 should be seen as a quick look forward because Darius came well before Xerxes. He is the king who features in the story of Esther in the book of the Bible by that name.

Artaxerxes (verse 7)
Artaxerxes I reigned over the Persian Empire 464–424BC, the period during which the story of Ezra and Nehemiah takes place. The date is not given, but by looking at Nehemiah 1:1–3 it would seem to be around 446BC, that is several years prior to his decree dated 444BC (Nehemiah 2:1–8).

Ashurbanipal (verse 10)
Osnappar is an alternative form of the name in the Aramaic. He became king of Assyria in 699BC on the death of his father Esarhaddon until his own death in about 626BC. It is thought that he was the king who liberated Manasseh from captivity in Nineveh (2 Chronicles 33:13). He captured the city of Susa in 645BC.

Ashurbanipal has since become famous as a result of excavations at Nineveh which revealed his great collection of literature on clay tablets. 30,000 tablets were discovered by George Smith from AD 1854 to 1873.

Ezra 5:1–5

Words and work

God's word can never be suppressed and he will be with those who do his will.

The work had come to a standstill, the builders were laid off – but not for long. God always has someone waiting for the right moment to get things moving again and Jerusalem at the time of Ezra was no exception. It was time to get back to work.

The two prophets Haggai and Zechariah make their appearance in order to encourage the people to get on with rebuilding the temple. Much of what they actually said and did is covered by the books of Haggai and Zechariah. It was a time of political upheaval and also a period when people were in danger of forgetting their commission to restore the temple and instead were looking after their own personal comfort. It was time to put words into consolidated action; Zerubbabel and Jeshua set the example. There is no use in telling others what to do unless you are prepared to get your own hands dirty, and so the prophets joined in the work (verse 2).

God had given permission, but as yet the civil authorities had not had the paperwork and so Tattenai, the provincial governor, asks, 'Who authorised you to rebuild this temple and restore this structure?' (verse 3). There appears to have been no hostility about his enquiry, but as far as he was concerned, he had not been informed through proper channels and so was checking things out for himself. Like so many administrators, he wanted to ensure he had covered himself in case there was any backlash from higher up.

However, God had his eye on things (verse 5) and the work continued. The phrase is worth noting because the more normal phrase used was 'the hand of God'. 'The eye of God' is a bit more rare (Job 36:7; Psalm 33:18; 34:15), but it was reassuring to know that God was watching. It may be a play on words because the Persian inspectors were known at that time as 'the king's eye'.

Sometimes people forget and think God comes and goes. This is why Jesus told the story of the Father noticing the sparrow which falls, and having such an eye for detail that even the hairs on our heads are numbered (Matthew 12:29–30; Luke 12:6–7).

The difficulty in the situation was the fact God had given permission to continue rebuilding but the civil authorities, it appeared, had not: there was still an order out that the work should cease (4:21). Encouraged by the two prophets, the Jews in Jerusalem made a hard choice: God's authority was final, this order had come right from the top! He was in charge of everything, including the civil authorities. Words must now be translated into work.

Throughout the centuries Christians have struggled with the same issues: what do you do when God tells you one thing and the civil authorities another, and how can you be sure that it is God who is speaking? Neither of these questions have easy answers and people have died believing God's will was more important than that of the state or even church government.

One thing is certain: if you talk too much, nothing gets done. Without vision people tend to form committees. People of vision are always marked by their eagerness to turn words into work under the certain conviction that the will of God will never be suppressed.

Questions

1. If you had to work out the percentage of time you spend talking and the time you spend working, what would be the split?
2. If you lived in a country where it was illegal to attend church and death was the penalty for breaking the law, what would you do, honestly?
3. Even in the church there is often more talk than action. This has resulted in people in the church getting on with a task without church approval (refusal to pay certain taxes, civil disobedience and violent resistance, for example). How do you think Christians should respond in the light of Paul's comments in Romans 13:1–6?

Personalities

Haggai (verse 1)

We do not know very much about Haggai although it seems certain from the text that he was well known at the time. His name is taken from the Hebrew word for 'a sacred festival'. It is by no means clear whether he had been in exile or whether he had stayed in Judah.

What we do know is that he prophesied to God's people, calling on them to stop looking after their own houses and neglecting the house of God, the temple (Haggai 1:4–6). He is called to speak on behalf of God at a time when there was a need to stir up the national conscience. In 520BC, within a three-month period, he spoke four times and then seems to disappear from public view. However, his words were certainly effective as they did stir people into action.

Ezra 5:6–17

Check it out!

Whenever the truth is questioned, it is important to discover the facts.

Tattenai, the Persian governor, then sent a letter to the king to inform him of events and establish the facts before making any move at all. He includes the  response given to him by the Jewish leaders when asked on whose authority the work had restarted (verses 11–16).

The word 'elders' is used in verse 9, but the more normal wording for leaders in Ezra is 'the heads of families' (Ezra 1:5; 3:12; 4:3) which suggests this is the actual wording used by Tattenai rather than a precis by Ezra. The list of names is not included (verse 10) and could mean one of two things: either they refused to give one, or it was a repeat list of those mentioned in Ezra 2.

The main appeal of the letter, as far as the Persian authorities were concerned, was the claim that a former king, Cyrus, had given permission for the temple to be restored. The king's word was law and the laws of the Persians and the Medes were unalterable. Darius would be under obligation to allow the work to continue if the truth could be established. Tattenai asks for a search to be made in the record office in order to discover the facts.

Too often mistakes are made because someone is not in possession of all the facts; Tattenai was taking no chances. Following on the last section, if Christians are seeking God's will, it is important to be aware of all the facts in a situation, otherwise people can go charging in like a bull in a china shop and cause more harm than good. Tattenai resorted to the Persian archives and the king for his authority. Believers have access to the highest authority, God's Word, and so it is important to ensure we have the backing of Scripture before embarking on what we believe is a God-given task. Sometimes the phrase 'God told me' is used as a shut-up bid by an individual in the church to over-ride the authority of the leadership. There may be a valid basis for their claim, but the only way to be sure of the truth is to test it. In the words of John, 'test the spirits to see whether they are from God' (1 John 4:1). Weigh it, pray it, search the Scriptures; in other words, check it out!

Questions

1. What ways do you have of checking out what God is saying to you as against your own personal desires?
2. How do creeds (statements of belief) help the church guard the truth?
3. When churches claim to have searched the Bible for answers and come to different conclusions, is there any other way of discovering the truth?

Geography

Chaldea (verse 12)

Chaldea is the name given to the southern part of Babylon and is also used of the semi-nomadic tribe who lived in the wilderness region between north Arabia and the Persian Gulf. The great city of Ur is referred to as Ur of the Chaldees (Genesis 22:22). Nebuchadnezzar was from the Chaldean tribe, but was also king of Babylon, and so the term is widened to mean all of Babylon (Isaiah 13:19; 47:1, 5; 48:14, 20).

Ezra 6:1–12

Mentioned in dispatches

It might seem easier just to ignore those in authority when there is conflict of interest, but it is always best to try and work through the system if you can.

Darius put his researchers to work in the treasury archives to discover if there was any truth in the claim made by the Jewish leaders in Jerusalem. A scroll was  found. The rebuilding of the temple was mentioned in despatches. In fact, even the building specifications were included, so there could be no argument (verses 3–5). Darius sent a letter back to Tattenai and proclaimed it a royal decree, informing him that there should be no interference and that the work should continue, with all expenses paid (verse 8). Just to show that he meant business, Darius included a pretty gruesome description of the fate of anyone foolish enough to ignore his decree (verses 11–12).

Imagine how Haggai and Zechariah would have felt when the news reached Jerusalem. They had proclaimed God's word in faith, convinced they were right. They had endured the administrative frustrations of civil government, going through correct procedures, and finally had discovered that patience really is a virtue, as well as a gift from God. There may have been a temptation to take short-cuts, but they resisted and did everything decently and in order. Now they not only had the king's consent, but cash from the royal treasury to cover costs as well!

Many years later, and speaking in the context of false prophecy and persecution, Jesus said, 'He who stands firm to the end will be saved' (Matthew 24:13; Mark 13:13).

Plodding through civil structure and administration to achieve the purposes of God can be one of the most irritating experiences in life, so why bother? Well, apart from the point that impatience is not exactly glorifying God, take the example of the patience of the Jews, not only in this story but over thousands of years. They have consistently proved that patient plodding works. It may not be easy, but you get there in the end.

Persecution and opposition to Christian activities sometimes seem to succeed in the short term. However, there is a way to overcome resistance to God's work, apart from patience. A person called Peter Marshall once said, 'Prayer moves the hand that controls the universe.' The builders of the temple must have been a people of prayer because Darius was keen to be mentioned in despatches to God. He asked in his letter to Tattenai that the priests 'pray for the well-being of the king and his sons' (verse 10). So he must have been impressed with their faith. Whenever you are involved in difficulties make sure it gets mentioned in despatches.

Questions

1. When you feel everything and everyone is against you because of your faith, what do you do in order to cope?
2. When you have prayed specifically for something or someone, what have been the longest and shortest times before you received an answer?
3. Church leaders in this country are sometimes criticized for not giving enough of a moral and ethical lead to the nation – how should they respond?

Ezra 6:13–16

Prescription for joy

There is real joy in seeing God's will completed, and knowing you are part of it is a real tonic.

Tattenai played it by the book. He had his instructions and there was no bad feeling. He made sure every assistance was available to complete the temple. Building work carried on and so did the preachers (verse 14), presumably during the tea-breaks!

The hopes and dreams of those who had returned home so many years before were fulfilled as the temple once again stood proudly over Jerusalem. It was completed on the third day of Adar, now widely accepted as 12 March 515BC. This marks Jeremiah's prophecy of seventy years (see chapter one) from the temple's destruction to its restoration.

After the fall of Jerusalem, and the deportations of many of the Jews, maintaining an identity would have been a real problem. It would have been even more difficult on return to discover strangers from other lands had moved into the area. Rebuilding the temple was a bit like raising the flag on a battleground. Now the temple had been completed, Jerusalem could once again be known as the Holy City, and Jews from all over the empire could look to it for their identity. It was a place which would focus on the presence of God. The completion of the temple was a real prescription for joy.

The foundation stone for the new temple was laid when Jesus became the capstone or cornerstone (1 Peter 2:7), and Peter reminds his readers at the beginning of the same chapter that every believer is a living stone being built into the temple. This theme of believers being built into a temple with Christ as the foundation occurs a number of times in the New Testament (1 Corinthians 3:16; 6:19; 2 Corinthians 6:16; Ephesians 2:20-21; Revelation 3:12; 21:22).

Commencing a new development can be exciting; continuing the task requires endurance; and completion of the work leads to blessing and job satisfaction. It is a good prescription for joy in the power and presence of God.

Questions

1. Have you ever been involved in a project from beginning to end? How did you feel when it was completed?
2. Do you think it is possible to be a Christian without belonging to a church? If your answer is 'Yes', where can such a person feel he or she belongs?
3. When will the building of the temple of Jesus Christ be completed?

Ezra 6:17-22

Cause for joy

Sacrificial giving to God and worship to him are a real cause for joy for the believer.

The feast of Passover was a memorial celebrating God's deliverance of his people from their first captivity in Egypt. Now it was cause of celebration for freedom, not only from slavery in Egypt but exile in Babylon. The cream on the cake, so to speak, was the opportunity to celebrate the completion of the temple as well. It was not quite on the same scale as the dedication of the first temple built by Solomon, because the nation was only just being re-established in the land. For instance, over two hundred times as many animals were sacrificed at Solomon's temple – compare verses 16–17 with 1 Kings 8:63.

People had given generously to the building fund when they could have put forward a case for their own needs but did not. It was not a question of how much was given but at what cost? This is very much reminiscent of the story of Jesus watching people putting their offerings into the temple treasury. Jesus measured the gifts not by the amount given but by the sacrifice involved: 'I tell you the truth, this poor widow has put more into the treasury than all the others. They gave out of their wealth; but she gave out of her poverty' (Mark 12:43–44).

Celebration involved not only the giving of sacrifices but also total giving of each individual of themselves to God. This is what purification involved (verse 20): getting rid of anything in their lives that was not acceptable to God in order to give themselves completely to him. This meant they were truly free to celebrate and the result was a seven-day-long 'knees up' because God filled them with joy (verse 22). There was nothing cold and formal about this time of worship; God had made them glad! The Hebrew word which is used for 'joy' means 'enjoying yourself', or 'having a good time'. Some might find it hard to imagine that God would give people the opportunity for a good time, a party atmosphere, in worship. (For more on the two main Hebrew concepts of joy see the comments on Nehemiah 8:9–12.)

The story has much of the feel of a birthday party: a party where a lot of time and planning have gone into making sure everything goes smoothly, where people have given almost beyond their ability to give because of their love for the one who is the reason for the celebration. The joy comes from the response of the person when they have opened the presents and joined in the party.

Jesus probably had something of this kind of merriment in mind when he spoke about the kingdom of God. He used parables which focused on banquets and weddings to explain that building the kingdom of God was a cause of real excitement for those who were prepared to make the effort. Tony Campolo, an American preacher and sociologist, says it well, 'The kingdom of God is a party!'

The point is well made in this passage that nothing comes from doing nothing, but giving personally of money, time and effort at a sacrificial level to God is ultimately a real cause for joy.

Questions

1. What kind of experiences make you happy?
2. How do you discern the difference between greed and need in your life?
3. What can the worldwide church learn from this passage?

Biblical terms

The book of Moses (verse 18)
'The book of Moses' and similar phrases ('the book of the covenant' and 'the Law of Moses') assume the reader is familiar with the rules and regulations of religious practice and community life as recorded in the first five books of the Bible (see Exodus 29; Leviticus 8 and Numbers 3:5–6; 8:5–6).

Times and seasons

Passover (verse 19)

The Feast of Passover is described in Exodus 12:6, Leviticus 23:5–6 and Numbers 9:11. On the day before Passover each Jewish household searched to make sure that there was no leavened bread (bread made with yeast) anywhere in the house. On the day itself a lamb or goat was taken to the temple for sacrifice (about one animal for every ten to twelve people), the fat was burned and the blood spilled onto the altar. The carcass was usually taken home and cooked. The ceremony that followed was a remembrance of the events leading up to the leaving of Egypt by the Israelites at the time of Moses and the exodus (the going out). Jews today will sometimes call it the Feast of Freedom.

Feast of Unleavened Bread (verse 22)

Instruction for this feast can be found in Exodus 12:15–20, Leviticus 23:6–8 and Numbers 28:17. As in 2 Chronicles 30:21 the emphasis of this feast is *joy* (vv. 16 and 22; see note on Ezra 3:12–13), to make clear that this is a very happy occasion.

The ceremony was enacted through a series of questions and answers led by the head of the household and prompted normally by the youngest articulate member of the family. In it they were reminded that the unleavened bread (bread made without yeast), bitter herbs and chutney symbolized the haste, the bitterness and the hard labour their ancestors had experienced in Egypt. Four cups of red wine were used to give thanks to God and only unleavened bread was eaten during that week.

Rebuilding God's people

Ezra 7:1 – 10:44

Ezra 7:1–10

Man with a mission

God always has the right person for the right time in history to help his people.

The first two stages in God's incredible plan, outlined in Ezra and Nehemiah, are now complete. His people have returned to the land and his temple has been restored. With the beginning of chapter 7 the third stage lifts off as Ezra, the man with a mission, comes onto the scene. His task? To begin to rebuild the people of God into a nation of spiritual power and purity for the sake of the glory of God.

This passage gives the reader a bit of background information regarding Ezra and his family tree. He arrives in Jerusalem sixty years on from the period covered by chapter 6 in 458BC. Ezra set out from the Jewish community in Babylon, with a letter from Artaxerxes I, to ensure that the Jews in Jerusalem and the surrounding area observed their religious laws in full. Ezra brought a significant number of people with him from Babylon (a journey of some nine hundred miles) to help in the task and also to make financial contributions for the temple.

Ezra is the Aramaic equivalent of the Hebrew name Azariah and means 'the Lord has helped'. His family tree listed here makes it clear that he has a good priestly pedigree, but he is not listed as a high priest. He is attributed with the authorship of Chronicles, Ezra and Nehemiah according to tradition.

Ezra is popularly known as 'Ezra the scribe'. For some reason which is not obvious, the NIV translates the Hebrew word used here as 'teacher' (verses 6 and 11) and yet,

speaking of the same person (Ezra) it translates the same
Hebrew word as 'scribe' in Nehemiah (8:1, 4, 9, and 13;
12:26 and 36). The word can also mean 'secretary'. By the
time of Ezra the Hebrew for 'to count' or 'to recount', had
come to mean 'one who is skilled in reading and inter-
preting religious writings and law' – a sort of court
scholar.

Until the exile scribes were separate from priests, but
Ezra was a scribe (teacher) as well as a priest, and probably advised King Artaxerxes on Jewish affairs. Scribes
were also employed as secretaries to write letters, legal
documents, and to keep records and accounts (Jeremiah
32:12; 36:26; 2 Chronicles 24:11). It was a financially
rewarding profession which often passed from father to
son (1 Chronicles 2:55).

Ezra's role was going to be a tough one. He was
expected to be a guardian of God's Word, both a priest
and a teacher of the Law (verse 6), devoted to its study
and observance (verse 10). The king of Persia obviously
had great faith in him because he gave him everything he
asked for. Twice in this short passage it is noted that
everything went well for Ezra because 'God's hand was
upon him' (verses 6 and 9). It is obvious to the reader that
Ezra is the man of the moment, a man with a mission. To
emphasize this the phrase is used again in 8:18, 22, 31.

Throughout the Bible there is a pattern which demonstrates the fact that God always has the right person for
the right time in history. Moses led the exodus, Joshua was
prepared for conquering Canaan, and David was ready
and waiting in the wings when Saul's rule failed. Right
through the Old Testament this pattern continued until
God called his own Son to carry out the ultimate mission,
to break the power of sin and death, to make it possible for
a lost world to be reconciled to its Maker. Then, after the
resurrection, came Peter, Paul, and many more men and
women who have all been part of God's incredible plan.

Most of those concerned did not think they were ready
or fit for the job, but God used them anyway. Jeremiah
comes close to understanding God's way when he writes

of Israel, 'Like clay in the hand of the potter, so you are in my hand' (Jeremiah 18:6), and Paul brings a Christian perspective, 'Does not the potter have the right to make out of the same lump of clay some pottery for noble purposes and some for common use?' (Romans 9:21). God always has the right person at the right place at the right time, even though the person often doesn't feel up to the task. But it is not a question of 'What can I do for God?' It is more a case of 'What can God do with me?'

Questions

1. How has God used you, and did you feel you were the right person?
2. Why do you think Ezra was not with the first group of Jews to return?
3. Who would you say is God's man or woman of the moment in the world today?

Ezra 7:11–26

In the name of the king

God places rulers in authority, so it should not surprise us to see kings being used to provide the way forward for God's will.

The significance of Ezra's part in God's plan is emphasized by the fact that not only had the king given him what he had asked for, but he had credentials in the form of a letter in the name of the king. In the letter Ezra is recognized by the king as a teacher of the law of

God (verse 12) and he is sent to Jerusalem by the king (verse 14) to check up on observance of the Law of God. 'The Law of God, which is in your hand' (verse 14) did not mean that he literally had a scroll of the Law, or Torah in his hand. 'In his hand' was a metaphor meaning that it was in his care and he understood it: hence the title given to Ezra in verse 11.

What is amazing is that the non-Jewish king tells Ezra to take money from the state treasury to finance his work in addition to the freewill offering (verse 16). The king asks him to be responsible not only for the Law of God, but the law of the king as well (verses 25–26). Appointing magistrates and judges on behalf of the king may well mean 'judges and officials', which would be very much in line with the Torah (Deuteronomy 16:18).

Some have debated whether Ezra actually had the king's authority over civil issues as well as the sacred and have suggested that really they were one and the same. The evidence suggests that as Jews living in Babylon had been subject to civil law for some years, it is perfectly reasonable to suppose the king gave Ezra authority over both civil and religious law. There are other examples of this, such as the Egyptian *satrap* who was given a similar brief by Darius in 519BC.[4]

Other Jews in Babylon had been given responsibility in affairs of state including Daniel and his friends, and Esther who became queen.

There have often been tensions between religion and politics, church and state, but then there have always been Christians who have also been involved in both. Like Ezra they could claim to be doing their job in the name of God and in the name of the king. The difficulty has always been to know where to draw the line between the law of the land and the Law of God. In Jesus' day the religious leaders tried to trap him on a number of occasions by getting him into debate on this very controversy: what belonged to God and what belonged to the civil ruler (Matthew 22:15–21)? When religious law and civil law were both broken, which had priority over the other?

If Jesus claimed to be a king, was he infringing on the authority of the Roman Empire?

The point of the passage is that God is in control. He has authority, even over rulers, and so can and does use them to carry out his will. How else did Ezra manage to obtain such an encouraging letter from Artaxerxes? That is why in reply to one trick question Jesus answered, 'Give Caesar what is Caesar's, and give to God what is God's' (Matthew 22:21). For this reason we still tend to include prayers for those in civil leadership and authority in church prayer books. The key to Ezra's mission and to ours is that whatever is done is carried out in the name of the King.

Questions

1. There is a saying which states, 'politics and religion don't mix'. What do you think?
2. If Christians are appointed as legal judges, have they the right to stand in judgment over others when the Bible tells us we must not?
3. Can you be a Christian and a politician?

Weights and measures

Talents, cors and baths (verse 22)
It is not easy to give the exact modern equivalent of these measurements because of the amount of flexibility in definition. For example, we know that the temple of Solomon had a large tank known as the 'sea of bronze'. According to 1 Kings 7:23–26 it contained 2,000 baths (3,000 in 2 Chronicles 4:5). A bath is a measure of liquids such as water, wine and oil (1 Kings 7:26 and 38; 2 Chronicles 2:9; Ezekiel 45:14) and a hundred baths is equal to roughly 607 gallons.

A hundred talents of silver would weigh approximately 3.75 tons. The 'cor' is used as a measure for flour, wheat and barley (1 Kings 5:2). A hundred cors of wheat would be around 650 bushels.

Ezra 7:27–28

Thanks a lot!

It is important not to take God for granted but to give him thanks always.

These few verses form a classic Hebrew benediction in the form of a psalm of praise, thanking God for his goodness and then giving an account of what he has done. It is a pattern which is followed again and again in the book of Psalms.

Ezra makes it clear here why he is God's man of the moment. He never forgets to give him thanks for the way he was working through the structures and in Ezra's own life. He happily acknowledges that he has achieved what he has only through the provision and intervention of the Lord: a God who can move a foreign king's heart to be concerned over Jerusalem and its temple. Armed with the knowledge that God is on his side, Ezra prepares to lead a caravan of Jewish leaders down to Jerusalem.

The use of the words 'his good favour' (verse 28) is a pity because the NIV has weakened the meaning of the Hebrew here. The word used for 'good favour' is normally translated 'care', 'loving kindness', 'mercy', or 'covenant love'. It comes from an Old Testament word for the stork, a bird devoted in its care for its young, and so 'the devoted or unchanging love of God for his people' is the intention behind the word. The most powerful illustration of its use is in the story of God's love for Israel in the book of Hosea (2:19; 4:1; 6:4, 6; 10:12; 12:6). The same word occurs in Ezra 3:11; 9:9 and Nehemiah 1:5; 9:17, 32; 13:14, 33.

Recognizing God's unchanging love and giving thanks for it is a constant theme in the Psalms. Daniel was a man of prayer who was known for the way he regularly gave thanks to God (Daniel 6:10). The frustration is that, human nature being what it is, we are usually far quicker at complaining when things are not right than in giving thanks when God's goodness is apparent. Jesus made this point when he healed the ten lepers. They were all quick enough to ask for help but only one bothered to come back and thank Jesus for what he had done (Luke 17:11–19).

I remember as a child that I loved getting presents for my birthday or for Christmas. What I was not so fond of was sitting down to write 'thank-you letters' afterwards. My mother pointed out that if I didn't, then I should not expect family and friends to send me anything. The principle is the same in the Christian life; if I take God for granted, do I have any right to expect him to help me? Surely it is a Christian's duty when he or she recognizes God's provision in life to say, 'Thanks a lot!'

Questions

1. What has God done for you today?
2. If you think about the prayers you have prayed recently, how many were 'I wants', and how many were 'thank yous'?
3. Why are people quicker to complain than to say 'thank you'?

Ezra 8:1–14

Role of honour

The list of names is a reminder that every one of us is known by name to God.

All of the families listed here, with the possible exception of Joab's (verse 9), are rejoining relatives who had returned eighty years earlier (Ezra 2:3–15; cf. 8:3–14). In Ezra 2:6 the family tree is taken directly from Pahath-Moab through Jeshua and Joab (this is not a family name but means 'governor of Moab'). Here, however, the main family is mentioned in verse 4 and Joab's family line is listed as a separate group. It may be because this is an easier way of breaking down the numbers involved or to single out Joab as different from the one mentioned in Ezra 2:6, it is not clear which.

The role of honour breaks down into three main groups, similar to other lists of names in Ezra and Nehemiah. First are the priests (verse 2) followed by the noble families (verses 2–3) and then those from ordinary families who make up the bulk of the caravan (verses 3–14). Some of the family names are also mentioned in the second chapter of Ezra which suggests that those who had gone back to Jerusalem on the first return had sent word to Babylon, and now more members of their families were setting out to join them.

The whole caravan, including men, women and children, would have probably numbered somewhere around 5,000 people. That Ezra had managed to recruit this many people suggests that a new sense of purpose and the presence of God was beginning to burn in the hearts of his people. The first return must have been compared with the exodus of Moses and the people from Egypt. Those families whose names were recorded in Ezra 2 had their names on the roll of honour, now others were following their example.

Something akin to the pioneering spirit of the people groups who left Europe to begin a new life in America or Australia in the nineteenth century must have gripped the Israelites. This excitement and desire to return to the promised land would affect the Jews of Russia in the latter part of the last century. It would gather momentum as Jews from France, Britain and Europe, then the rest of the world, began to experience the same feeling that God was calling them home to the land of Israel, until Israel was a nation once again with Jerusalem as its capital.

One thing worth noting is that there are no lists of families in Babylon other than those who return to Israel. There is no criticism of which group returned when, it was only important that they returned. Then their names were placed on the role of honour.

This event has some similarity with the Christian call to return to a right relationship with God through Jesus Christ. It doesn't matter when someone returns to God, only that they do return. Then their names can be included on the role of honour – the Lamb's book of life (Philippians 4:3; Revelation 3:5; 13:8; 17:8; 20:12, 15; 22:14).

Questions

1. Why do churches sometimes put people's names on memorial plaques in their buildings?
2. Do you think it is easier to be a Christian if you already have family in the church?
3. When the prodigal son returned home (Luke 15:11–32) why did the brother and the father have different attitudes?

Biblical terms

The last ones (verse 13)

This phrase has puzzled some scholars a bit because the main pattern of listing the families changes at this point. Some have suggested that these words were added later, others that it just meant 'and finally'. There is another possibility, however: this family could have been making 'aliyah'.

This is a Hebrew word which literally means 'going up' and was used in a number of ways: for example, going up to the lectern to read a portion of Scripture, or of an upper room. But it is also used to mean 'returning to Palestine'. The phrase is used in Ezra 1:3 and 5 in just this way. The call 'to go up' and possess the land is the same word (Deuteronomy 9:23).

So 'the last ones' could well be the last members of that family to make their *aliyah* back to Palestine, as against the large numbers of Jews who never returned.

Ezra 8:15–20

Down by the riverside

Being where God wants you to be means being prepared to do your duty.

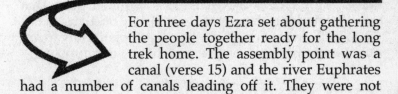

For three days Ezra set about gathering the people together ready for the long trek home. The assembly point was a canal (verse 15) and the river Euphrates had a number of canals leading off it. They were not narrow-boat canals but drainage canals used to defend the fields against flooding. Both the Tigris and Euphrates rivers were subject to flooding in the early summer and waiting for the waters to go down would have meant it was too late for seed sowing. In order to tackle the problem a whole series of canals or dykes were dug for drainage. The same word is used in Psalm 74:15 referring to 'streams' and Psalm 93:3 where the word used is 'flood' (RSV) or 'sea' (NIV), reflecting the idea of water that comes and goes. I wonder if this is where the hymn-writer got the idea for the hymn, 'Shall we gather at the river?'

When Ezra came to check out the mix of people who made up the caravan, he discovered a shortage of Levites. As one of the primary reasons for the return was to build up the Jews of Israel in their relationship with God, it was vital to have a reasonable number of religious leaders. There were priests (verse 15), men of learning (verse 16), and temple servants (verse 20), but no Levites. Building the temple was one thing, but trying to maintain a believing body of people without proper leadership was quite another. Ezra knew that they must be prepared, even if the hand of God was on them (verse 18).

Sometimes when believers are faced with practical difficulties they fall into the trap of saying, 'God is with us, so everything will work out fine,' but make no attempt to do anything themselves. Ezra seems to have worked on the principal that 'the Lord helps those who help themselves', as we shall see later. Part of real spirituality is to ensure practical details are dealt with in a realistic rather than fatalistic way. Ezra ensured he had everything and everyone he needed before he was prepared to embark on the mission God had called him to.

The motto of the scout movement is, 'Be prepared!', and one of the promises they make is to do their duty. That was the model of Ezra and the call to Christians today. God is with us, but don't see that as an opportunity to opt out of responsibility – be prepared to do your duty.

Questions

1. What do think might have happened if Ezra had set off, failing to notice that he had no Levites?
2. Do you know people who leave everything to God to sort out without making any effort themselves?
3. How should the church ensure an eye for detail as well as carrying out its commission?

Ezra 8:21–31

Fasting and faith

Prayer and fasting are part of seeking God's will and purpose. They help those who believe to go forward in faith.

At the Ahava canal everything from the practical planning to the spiritual preparation was being organized – or was it? Ezra did not feel able to ask for the king's protection because he had made it clear God was looking after them (verse 22). It was really a case of faith without works is dead. Ezra could not claim God was on his side if he was not prepared to prove it by his actions. This is probably why he proclaimed the fast (verse 21).

Fasting is mentioned only three times in Ezra–Nehemiah (Ezra 8:21–23; Nehemiah 1:4; 9:1). Each time there is a direct link between fasting and conversation with God, and it normally meant abstaining from food and drink for a time. In this context it is preparatory to the request of a safe journey for the families and their belongings as they set out from Babylon to Jerusalem. There were set fast-days during the year, such as the 'Day of Atonement' or 'Yom

Kippur' (Leviticus 16:29, 31; 23:27–32), and there were also one-off fasts for groups and individuals such as the examples found in Ezra and Nehemiah.

Fasting was used to express sorrow over sin and misfortune as well as displaying humility before God and people. Often fasting was perceived as a way of beginning to discover God's will for a particular situation, but there was always the warning that it was a waste of time if right living did not accompany it (Isaiah 58:3–12; Matthew 6:16–18). In the Matthew account it is interesting to note that Jesus assumes that fasting is a part of the normal spiritual life. He does not say, 'If you fast', but, 'When you fast' (verse 16). Ezra needed to be sure of God's will if they were to have a safe journey (verse 21), especially in view of the large amount of valuables they would be carrying (verses 25–27). The words mean literally 'a straight road', which is interesting when you compare Isaiah's and John the Baptist's words (Isaiah 40:3–4, Mark 1:3). The English language has something of this sense in its use of 'straight' or 'crooked' (that is, good or bad) to describe people.

I feel a bit sorry for the priests because they, and not some strong armed fighters, were given specific responsibility for guarding the gifts for the temple. However, the responsibility probably improved their inclination to fast and pray! True to form, being prepared to do his duty, and always practical in his eye for essentials, Ezra assisted the priests over any temptation to help themselves to the temple treasure by weighing it out before handing it over (verses 25–27). He would weigh it again when they arrived in Jerusalem (verse 33). The fasting and faith were rewarded because God protected them from bandits along the way (verse 31).

Ezra demonstrates an important fact for Christians: being spiritual does not mean being naïve or taken for a fool. At the same time, it is essential that faith is in God and not human institutions. I like the old saying, 'We trust the Lord, everybody else pays cash.' Know God's will then do it, and in order to be certain follow the model given by Ezra: fasting and faith.

Questions

1. How can someone with specific dietery needs (such as a diabetic) fast without being irresponsible?
2. Why does going without food help us focus on God?
3. Should the church encourage fasting as a regular part of worship today?

Biblical terms

You ... are consecrated to the LORD (verse 28)
Consecrated is another word for holy. The Hebrew means 'sacred', 'set apart' (for a purpose), 'dedicated to' or 'for', 'consecrated', 'holy', 'sanctified' and implies something or someone who is free from defilement or impurity (Ezra 3:5; Nehemiah 3:1; 8:9, 10, 11; 10:39; 12:47; 13:22). With it comes the expectation of being ceremonially clean in order to come into the presence of God (Leviticus 16:4, 16–33).

Ezra 8:32–36

Return and rest

No-one is expected to keep going non-stop – rest is just as important as action.

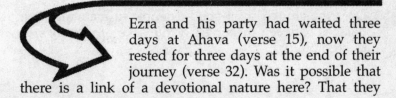

Ezra and his party had waited three days at Ahava (verse 15), now they rested for three days at the end of their journey (verse 32). Was it possible that there is a link of a devotional nature here? That they waited not only for the Levites, but also to follow the pattern of the first exodus?

If we go by the calendar in the Book of Jubilees (which gives a chronology of the main events of Israel's history to the day of the week), then it is feasible that they arrived back on the eve of the sabbath (the day of rest), the same day of the week that Joshua had entered the land of Canaan, when he also paused for three days (Joshua 3:1). As a result, it would not be possible to deliver up the valuables they had brought with them to the priest at Jerusalem for three days.

This apart, three days was regarded as a normal rest period during this time (Ezra 10:8; Nehemiah 2:11) and would be reasonable if you have to find food and shelter for around five thousand fellow travellers.

There is a warning in Psalm 127:2 to workaholics: working all hours without proper rest is a waste of time because it is not God's intention. Even Jesus emphasized the need to take time for rest and relaxation (Matthew 11:28; 26:45; Mark 6:31). People sometimes feel guilty about taking time to rest and relax, but at the end of work it is not only in order, but an order from God.

Without proper rest after the return Ezra, and the people with him, would not have been in a fit state to continue the task God had set before them. The message has not changed – rest is as important as action.

Questions

1. How do you discern the difference between rest and being lazy?
2. Why do you think it is that some people never seem to take time to relax?
3. Does the church set a good example in maintaining a balance between meetings for the sake of meetings or doing nothing?

Personalities

Meremoth (verse 33)

This person was the son of Uriah and belonged to the Hakkoz family. He is also mentioned in Nehemiah 3:4–21. The Hakkoz family was one of those which, on the first return, were not able to prove they were of good Jewish stock (Ezra 2:59–63). Obviously someone must have sorted something out because now one of the leading priests is from this family.

Jozabad (verse 33)

Jozabad is a descendant of one of the families involved in the first return (Ezra 2:40) and an overseer of the outside work on the temple (Nehemiah 11:15).

Ezra 9:1–7

Crisis of faith

No-one can serve two masters, it only leads to conflict.

Ezra 9 and 10 form one complete section dealing with the issue of compromising relationships amongst the Jews. The people had returned to a confusing climate in which it was hard to discover their identity. On the one hand, there was a political structure which involved people from other nations and demanded their participation. On the other hand, there was a religious institution which also made demands on their loyalty to its requirements. The only way many had coped with this crisis of identity was to compromise, and compromise always seems to lead to conflict.

The leaders in Jerusalem obviously had a guilty conscience about the situation because soon after Ezra's arrival in the city they came and told him (rather like a child who has done wrong who takes the initiative and confesses before it is found out). Ezra's reaction was nothing if not dramatic. 'I tore my tunic … pulled hair from my head …' (verse 3). Behaviour of this kind was an expected reaction to bereavement (2 Samuel 13:19; 2 Kings 22:11; Job 1:20; Ezekiel 7:18). Tearing of clothes was a Jewish modification of going naked, as people of other nations might do in the same circumstances. Nakedness was viewed by Jewish religious law as a lack of dignity and seen as a mark of shame (Genesis 9:23; Ezekiel 16:39) or extreme poverty (Job 24:10), but tearing one's clothes was acceptable.

Men clipping their beards or shaving their heads in times of mourning was frowned on and priests were not expected to trim their beards at all (Leviticus 19:27; 21:5; Deuteronomy 14:1). The only parallel with Ezra's behaviour in this respect is Nehemiah 13:25 where Nehemiah pulled out the hair of some of the men of Judah as a punishment. One of the Hebrew words for 'elder' means literally 'someone capable of growing a beard', so to remove facial hair was symbolic of taking away authority (see Ezra 10:6). Ezra's act was typical of prophetic symbolism, usually an act of extreme behaviour to make a significant impact on God's people in times of apathy or ignorance (1 Samuel 19:24; Isaiah 20:1–4; Ezekiel 4 and 5).

Ezra records, 'I fell on my knees with my hands spread out' (verse 5). This was not the only position for prayer in the Old Testament (Exodus 9:29; 1 Kings 8:22; Isaiah 1:15). It was also permissible to pray standing (1 Samuel 1:26), kneeling (1 Kings 8:54), hands lifted up (Nehemiah 8:6), sitting (1 Chronicles 17:16) or even flat on one's face (1 Chronicles 21:16)! Praying on his knees, for Ezra, was a sign of submission (Psalm 95:6; Daniel 6:10). What he says makes it clear that he viewed their guilt as his guilt because he talks about 'our sins' (verse 6) and 'our guilt' (verse 7). Compromise had led to conflict and a crisis of faith. His attitude was not a condescending judgment but reaction out of corporate accountability.

We can learn from Ezra's response by resisting the temptation to look down on other Christians who have been caught in this trap and recognizing that, as a part of the body of Christ, we have to talk about *our* sins and *our* guilt – not just *theirs*.

Jesus recognized the problem and proclaimed, 'No man can serve two masters: for either he will hate the one, and love the other; or else he will be devoted to one and despise the other' (Matthew 6:24, Luke 16:13). Anything which gets between the Lord and a believer is idolatry, and the second commandment clearly condemned this practice (Exodus 20:4). When people attempt to water down the requirements of the Christian life, compromise will produce conflict – conflict of interest and identity. It will also result in a crisis of faith.

Questions

1. Can you think of examples of compromise which are testing the church today?
2. Are there things which come between you and God?
3. What can we do to help Christians who are trapped in compromise and caught up in a crisis of faith?

Biblical terms

Wives (verse 2)
The word 'wife' or 'wives' does not actually appear in the Hebrew; the phrase used means 'to lift up', 'to receive' or

'take up' and is used again in verse 12 and 10:44. It is used in Ezra 5:15 of taking vessels to the temple. So where the NIV suggests 'they have taken some of their daughters as wives' it is only implied and could equally be 'concubines' or 'cohabiters'. If the women taken were not wives but concubines it would make more sense of the situation in chapter 10 because it was easier to get rid of a concubine than a wife (Genesis 21:10–14).

Ezra 9:8–15

The righteous remnant

No matter what happens, God will always make sure that there are those who will be saved.

After the initial shock of the news of the state of the nation Ezra embarks on a prayer which is a mixture of confession and intercession for God's people to return to a right relationship with him. There is mention of 'detestable practices' (verse 11). This is a direct reference to the list in Deuteronomy 18:9–12 involving witchcraft, divination and child sacrifices.

A new word makes its sole appearance in Ezra in this chapter (verses 8, 14 and 15) and once at the beginning of Nehemiah (Nehemiah 1:2). The Hebrew word can be translated 'deliverance', 'escape', 'survive' or 'remainder'. It picks up an important piece of biblical theology which is echoed consistently throughout both the Old and New Testaments – that whatever else happens, there will always be a righteous remnant who God will save from destruction.

When Lot was captured someone escaped to tell Abraham (Genesis 14:13); Isaiah gives God's promise to king Hezekiah that a remnant of the house of Judah will survive (2 Kings 19:30–31) and the opening chapter of Nehemiah speaks of the remnant who have survived the exile.

In the New Testament the Greek words used in Romans 9:27 and 11:5 have the same underlying meaning. The remnant are that group of people who have remained faithful to God and his covenant despite the surrounding pressures and problems of life. The promise of God that there will always be a remnant who remain in any given situation has the implication of judgment and hope; God will preserve. It is first made clear in the story of Noah (Genesis 6:5). Joseph's life was preserved by God (Genesis 45:5); and Elijah was reminded of the righteous remnant (1 Kings 19:18). Other examples are the holy stump cut off to grow again (Isaiah 6:13), and the name of Isaiah's son *Shear Yashub*, which means 'a remnant shall return' (Isaiah 7:3).

Jesus becomes the remnant of one, then the church with Christ as head. That does not mean that everybody who belongs to a church will be included. Jesus himself made it clear that some would have a surprise when judgment day came (Matthew 7:21; 25:31–46; Luke 6:46; 13:25). Those who do his will and try to live the life of faith will be the righteous remnant.

Questions

1. Some people say that everybody will go to heaven in the end. Do you think that is true?
2. Who is in a position to say they are part of the righteous remnant?
3. Why did God allow the Jews to be taken from their land in the first place?

Biblical terms

A firm place (verse 8)
The actual word used is 'tent peg' and implies a place where a tent can be securely pitched. There are also links with the Tabernacle, or tent of meeting, which was pitched with bronze tent pegs (Exodus 27:19; 35:18; Numbers 3:37).

The New Jewish Publication Society translates this as 'and given us a stake in His holy place'. So the temple is seen as a safe place for the remnant.

A wall of protection (verse 9)
Some have used this as an argument for Nehemiah coming before Ezra and his wall already being in place. But it is a metaphor and not intended to be taken literally, otherwise it would surround not only Jerusalem but the whole of Judah.

The nation Israel is often likened to a vineyard and it is likely that the image of a wall is a vineyard wall (Psalm 80:12; Isaiah 5:5) rather than a city wall.

Ezra 10:1–4

Time to act

When people are really sorry for wrong-doing, talk alone is not enough – actions speak louder than words.

Ezra's prayer in chapter 9 is in his own words. Here the account changes to the third person and reflects the fact that the events of both Ezra and Nehemiah are drawn from a number of sources.

The results of Ezra's passionate prayer for the people led him to tears and he threw himself down (verse 1). The drama of Ezra's actions may seem a little odd to a Western reader, but this was a very acceptable way of expressing extreme grief in the Middle East. The use of the word 'throwing' or 'falling down' as part of worship is paralleled in the story of the fiery furnace in Daniel when the king demands that the three Hebrew young men fall down to his idol (Daniel 3:10–11, 15). This same word 'falling down' used in relation to an idol occurs in Isaiah 44:15 and 17. The same use of a parallel Greek word can be found in the New Testament (Matthew 4:9; 1 Corinthians 14:25).

It is hardly surprising that a large crowd gathered in response to Ezra's dramatic deliberations. His passion must have been powerful because it resulted in the men, women and children who were present weeping bitterly with him. Then Shecaniah, son of Jehiel, calls for practical action; it was time to act! 'Now let us make a covenant before our God …' (verse 3). There are two main words in Hebrew normally translated 'covenant'. The one used here (verse 3) can also mean 'treaty'. It is the only time it is used in Ezra and occurs four times in Nehemiah (Nehemiah 1:5; 9:8, 32; 13:29).

The same word is used when God establishes his covenant with Noah (Genesis 6:18), with Abraham (Genesis 15:18), with Moses and the Israelites (Exodus 19:5), and with King David and his descendants (2 Chronicles 13:5). The actual word normally associated with this idea is 'to cut a covenant', based on the religious rite of killing an animal and cutting it into two or three parts. Part of the animal was burnt as an offering and part was eaten in a religious meal sealing the covenant. This way of agreeing a covenant is found not only in the Bible (Genesis 15:17; Exodus 24:8; Jeremiah 34:18) but also in a number of ancient Near Eastern texts including the Mari texts (20,000 clay tablets found on the west bank of the Euphrates) and the Alalakh tablets (found at Tel Atchana near the Turkish/Syrian border). Deuteronomy 29:9–14 refers to the cutting of a covenant involving women and children.

The blood of Jesus is symbolized in wine when Jesus refers to it as the cup of the new covenant. The Greek word for 'covenant', 'testament' or 'will' (1 Corinthians 11:25) is used in speaking of the new relationship between God and those who believe through the sacrifice of his son.

The covenant is always initiated by God, and Jesus reminds us of this in John 15:15, 'You did not choose me, I chose you.' It is not a covenant between equals but, like a treaty after a war, between a strong party and a weak party. A covenant with God is not a contract which you can opt out of by giving notice (Joshua 9:3–15; 1 Samuel 11:1–2; 1 Kings 20:34). There are one or two instances of covenants with individuals but it is always with the wider community of God's people in mind (Jeremiah 32:36–40). The purpose of the covenant is mission (sending out the message of God) so that Israel is seen as a covenant for mission to the rest of the world (Isaiah 49:8).

The call to action was a tough one: making a covenant entailed sending away all foreign women from Jewish households, and their children as well (verse 3). Sexual encounters with foreigners had always been forbidden and now those who had been disobedient were about to pay the price.

'Talk is cheap' and 'Actions speak louder than words' are popular sayings with significant truths behind them. If I say to someone. 'I love you,' and then take no notice of that person, what do the words prove? It is easy to say, 'I am a Christian,' but what impression will that have on other people unless I practise what I preach? When things go wrong and life gets in a mess as a result of stupid behaviour and disobeying God, there is a time to confess wrong actions, a time to cry, but finally there comes a point when it is time to act.

Questions

1. What do you think about men crying and why?
2. Do you feel it is right to break up families because of religion?
3. How can the church act to show it means what it says?

Personalities

Shecaniah (verse 2)

Shecaniah is a lay person who appears to be a leader of the people because of his willingness to follow Ezra's lead in confessing the guilt of the Jewish community. His lead produces an effective and positive response from the crowds gathered round.

Biblical terms

Foreign women (verse 2)

The phrase in either the singular or plural recurs six times in Ezra 10 (10:2, 10, 14, 17, 18, 44) and nowhere else.

A number of prominent Old Testament men were married to foreign women, including Esau who married two Hittites (Genesis 26:34), Joseph who married an Egyptian (Genesis 41:45), Moses who married a Midianite (Exodus 2:21), David who married a Calebite and an Aramean (2 Samuel 3:3) and Solomon who married Moabites, Ammonites, Edomites, Sidonians and Hittites for wealth and to establish political treaties (2 Kings 11:1; 14:21). These mixed marriages were of great concern because they took away from Jewish purity of blood and were seen as a threat to religious faith (1 Kings 11:4). The

87

practice was actually forbidden by Jewish law (Exodus 34:15–16; Deuteronomy 7:3–4). The exception seems to be women captured in time of war, as long as they abandoned their original nationality (Deuteronomy 21:10–14).

The problem was that many just ignored these prohibitions when it suited them. It is borne out here (see Nehemiah 10:31; 13:23–27; Malachi 2:11–12).

Marrying (verse 2)

The same word recurs in verses 10, 14, 17 and 18 and although translated 'to marry' literally means 'to sit down' or 'sit still'. Often translated 'to live', 'inhabit', 'endure', 'remain', 'stay' it can also mean 'to cohabit'. It is only used in the sense of marriage here and in Nehemiah 13:23 and 27, although the actual word is used elsewhere in Ezra and Nehemiah in its more literal sense (Ezra 2:70; Nehemiah 3:26; 4:12; 7:73; 8:14; 11:1–4, 6, 21 and 25; and 13:16).

Normally the much stronger Hebrew word meaning 'to be master' or 'owner' is used for marriage (for example, Exodus 21:3; Deuteronomy 22:22; 24:1; Proverbs 30:23; Isaiah 54:1; 62:4 and 5; Jeremiah 3:14 and Malachi 2:2).

Ezra 10:5–11

Make up your mind

The choice is always there, God's will or self-interest. Sometimes it's a tough choice.

The response of Ezra to Shecaniah's call to a new covenant was immediate. He was quick to seize the opportunity and to ensure that this desire for a return to a right relationship with God was not lost in a cooling of passion. He called priests, leaders and people to make a public promise to put their words into action. Oaths (verse 5) had the same courtroom imagery then as they do today (Numbers 5:11–31; 1 Kings 8:31). It was seen as a religious test, but if a person refused to take the oath it was to accept guilt and was linked to those who refused to be witnesses (Leviticus 5:1).

In Hebrew 'to take an oath' or 'to make a covenant' literally means 'to use a curse'. That is, 'if I break this vow may this curse come upon me' (1 Samuel 14:24). Ezekiel 17:13–21 gives an account of an oath taken to seal a treaty (covenant) and the consequences of breaking it.

Jesus also took a very strong position on vows or oaths (Matthew 5:33–37). As a result, some religious groups today, like the Society of Friends, will not take the oath of allegiance or courtroom oath. When Jesus was asked by the high priest, under oath, if he was the messiah he said, 'Yes', but the high priest could not accept it, tore his clothes and accused him of blasphemy (Matthew 26:63).

Just in case anybody had second thoughts, Ezra had a proclamation sent to every area of Jerusalem and Judah (verse 7). It was definitely make-your-mind-up time! Anyone who failed to act according to the oaths of the gathering at the temple would be excluded from the assembly of the exiles (verse 8). Ezra gave the men (it was the men who had to make the decision in that culture) three days to gather in Jerusalem (verse 9). Such was the impact on the nation that the book of Ezra records that by the deadline 'all the people were sitting in the square before the house of God' (verse 9). If those who had cohabited with foreign women did not feel bad enough, now it began to rain. It never rains but when it pours!

The word for rain (verse 9) used here and in verse 13 implies very heavy downpours rather than just the odd shower. The rainy season usually began mid- to late-October but might not start in earnest until the beginning of January. The final rains were normally over by the end of April, or the beginning of May. If Ezra's public reading is the one recorded in Nehemiah 8 the date is the twentieth of Kislev. This would be sometime during the third week in December when it would not only be wet but also very cold because it would be mid-winter.

Downpours of rain were used as an illustration of blessings being poured down on the kingdom by its king (Psalm 72:6–7) or waiting for the coming of the Messiah (James 5:7). I doubt the people in the square were feeling blessed as they gathered there.

Have you ever noticed that most of the choices Scripture puts before Christians are tough ones? They are usually made worse because the call to come clean is often the result of our own stupidity. Even if it is not, the call to choose is no easier than that of the quizmaster who asks, 'Do you want to take the money or take a chance?' The main difference is that even when Christians feel they are under a cloud they can still be confident of the promise, '... in all things God works for the good of those who love him, who have been called according to his purpose.' (Romans 8:28). The conditions are obedience and the call to make up your mind.

Questions

1. Does your church tradition require you to make public promises, and if so, does it make it easier or harder for you to keep them?
2. If your church leadership make promises on your behalf, are you prepared to back them by acting on those promises?
3. What do you think about non-Christians making promises in a church building for the sake of a ceremony, but who obviously have no intention of keeping them?

Ezra 10:12–44

The great divorce

Life gets complicated when you go against God's will and it is harder to undo things than not to have done them in the first place.

The climax of the book of Ezra is quite tragic: the people responded positively to his call to separate themselves from the unbelievers, saying 'You are right! We must do as you say' (verse 12). But it was still a painful parting. A similar situation had occurred when Abraham tried to work out God's will for him and Sarah by taking her servant, Hagar, in order to produce a son. God did as he had promised and, against all the odds, Sarah produced a son, Isaac. Then Hagar and her son, Ishmael, were banished from the tribe (Genesis 21:1–10).

'We have sinned greatly in this thing' (verse 13). With a few notable exceptions the people accept Ezra's challenge and confess their guilt. 'We have sinned greatly' is the phrase used, but the actual sin is implied rather then stated. Even in Ezra's dramatic outburst his concern is the fact that people were breaking the covenant (Ezra 9:10–12) and risking bringing down God's anger and judgment (Ezra 9:14). This is more than just getting rid of foreign women. It is about the purification and separation of God's people for his will and purpose (see verse 11) in order to avoid divine retribution.

The word translated as 'thing' in verse 13 is from the Hebrew for 'to speak', and the implication is that God's word has been spoken. The power of God's word is reflected in Genesis 1 where God's word brought creation into being. 'The word of the LORD' is the voice of authority

(Ezra 1:1). John picks this up when he makes it clear that Jesus is 'the Word made flesh' (John 1:14). In the Hebrew mind God's word and his activity are one and the same and not to be separated. His people are intended to be a reflection of this.

Divorce was not part of God's original intention for his people (Genesis 2:24) and the only reason it was ever allowed was because of Israel's hardness of heart (Matthew 19:8; Mark 10:5; cf. Deuteronomy 24:1–4). Malachi makes it clear that God hates divorce but disobedience to the covenant is just as unacceptable (Malachi 2:16). Like naughty children, those who don't conduct themselves in a godly way will always end up having to pay the price for disobedience. Even King David found this out to his cost (2 Samuel 12:13–14).

The decision was a tough one for the nation of Israel, but obedience was vital if they were to maintain their identity as God's covenant people. The alternative was to go the way of those who water down the will of God and lose their identity in him. Those who had been caught in compromise had their names posted for all to see in the same way that shopkeepers of the 1930s depression in Britain put the names of bad debtors in their shop windows. The sad situation was resolved on 4 August (see Ezra 7:9). This meant that the whole unhappy business took about seventy-five working days.

Whenever the church of Jesus Christ has tried to act other than in obedience to God's Word it has declined to the point where it has become difficult to see where the ways of the world end and the position of the church begins. The Reformation was necessary because the church was no longer conducting itself according to the will of God, and the great divorce of the church began. Since then, many other denominations have arisen in response to the call to get back to the place where Jesus wants his people to be. Sadly, history demonstrates that each in turn has had to make the same journey as those Jews gathered at the temple with Ezra – return to God's way or disappear.

The lesson to be learned is this: don't do it in the first place and then you won't have to endure the painful process of undoing it. Disobeying Jesus' teachings results only in complications.

Questions

1. What examples of unholy alliances can you think of in the worldwide church today?
2. How far can we go as Christians in working alongside people who do not share our faith before we have to draw the line?
3. What is your reaction to churches who refuse to marry people who have been divorced?

Personnel

Elders and judges
'Elders' are mentioned also in Ezra 5:5, 9; 6:7, 8, 14, but not in Nehemiah. The particular word for elder used here and in verse 8 comes from the Hebrew for 'beard'. In Ezra 9:3 it is used of someone who is old, an elder, or chief magistrate. The elders had authority in civil affairs and assisted the chief priests in enforcing religious law amongst the clans identified with the towns and villages in Israel. They were also active during the exile (Ezekiel 8:1; 14:1; 20:1 and 3).

'Judges' – different Hebrew words are used in Ezra 4:9 and 7:25. The word used here is not found in this context anywhere else in Ezra or Nehemiah. The Hebrew word is used of someone who has the responsibility of governor or magistrate, someone who decides or defends.

Persian judges and magistrates of the same period were called 'law bearers' and had the responsibility of advising on the law of the land, but the final decision rested with the king. Darius was called 'the Law giver' by the peoples he ruled over. The Persians operated two kinds of court systems, one for dealing with family and property disputes, the other with taxation and crimes against the crown. In order to carry out this law, scribes were used and it may be that Ezra carried out this legal state function as well as his religious role.

Times and seasons

The first day of the tenth month (verse 16)
It is estimated that this was 29 December 458BC, ten days after Ezra's commission was established. The tenth month being Tebeth which was December/January, the time of rain and snow when sowing crops began.

Catching the vision

Nehemiah 1:1 – 2:20

Nehemiah 1:1–3

Dire straits

Freedom from captivity is not enough – it's what happens afterwards that counts.

Nehemiah was still working in Babylon when his brother Hanani brought news from the home country about the state of Jerusalem. The problems on the surface were of a physical nature, but underlying everything else was the spiritual state of things. The people of God who had returned home to rebuild with so much enthusiasm had now lost the vision. They were in dire straits; the big issue was why, and what could Nehemiah do about it?

The same story has been repeated throughout the history of God's people. When people have been close to God there has been a vision, an enthusiasm and energy to carry out his will and purpose. When the focus of life changes to personal desire, accumulation of wealth and legalism, the spiritual temperature goes down to luke-warm. The result is apathy and a downward spiral into a state of desperation which eventually turns individuals, churches and nations back to God. The book of Judges is full of examples of this pattern. The sadness is that each generation normally fails to learn from the mistakes of its predecessors. So God's people have to relearn the lesson of the need for God-centred lives and the restoration of biblical values in order to bring love, justice, dignity and direction, first to the church, and then to society.

Nehemiah needed Hanani to tell him about Jerusalem. Paul wrote, 'how can they hear without someone preaching to them' (Romans 10:14), but would Paul have been used to tell people about Jesus if Barnabas had not gone to tell him about the need of the church at Antioch (Acts 11:25)?

Paul told the crowd at Lystra that God never left himself without a witness to his love and concern for his creation (Acts 14:17). All who have discovered the saving power of Jesus are called upon to carry the message of good news, especially when the church is in dire straits.

Questions

1. Has God used someone to speak to you recently? If so, what was your experience?
2. Do you have a vision for God's will for your situation?
3. What has God set your church free from and why?

Personalities

Nehemiah (verse 1)
The name means 'the Lord (*Yahweh*) has comforted'. This is an interesting comparison with his father's name, Hacaliah, which means either 'the Lord is hidden' or 'wait for the Lord'. Nehemiah is mentioned in the Bible only in the books of Ezra and Nehemiah, however he is also acknowledged in writings such as 2 Maccabees 1:18–36 in the Apocrypha, and Jesus Sirach 48:13 as one who played a major part in the Feast of Tabernacles and the founding of a library. More than half this book is a personal diary of Nehemiah's experiences.

He was King Artaxerxes' cupbearer (see the note on verse 11) in 445BC and later was appointed governor (2:11). He returned to Persia in 433BC after the walls of Jerusalem had been rebuilt (5:14; 13:6). Nehemiah did come back to Jerusalem later on (13:7) but we can't be sure of the date.

The Talmud[5] (a Jewish commentary on the Bible) says that Nehemiah had a short temper and was full of his own self-righteous. This seems a little unkind, and we cannot be certain that it is true.

However, it is reasonable to make some assumptions about him based on the experiences of Daniel and his friends in Babylon. Nehemiah would probably be well trained (Daniel 1:4–5) and most likely quite good looking (Daniel 1:4, 13, 15). He would need to know about wines and, being frequently in the presence of the king, was in a position of some influence (see the note on verse 11).

Hanani (verse 2)

He was probably Nehemiah's real brother, although the word 'brother' was used sometimes to mean 'a male relative'. Later he was appointed as Nehemiah's deputy and put in charge of the citadel at Jerusalem (7:2) which supports the view that he was his brother.

The name Hanani means 'the Lord has been gracious' – another variation is Hananiah – and was quite a common name in Old Testament times.

Geography

The citadel of Susa

Referred to by its Hebrew name 'Shusan' in some versions, it was the spring residence of the Persian kings. Situated about 150 miles north of the Persian Gulf, it was one of the five capitals of the empire. The other four were Babylon, Parsagae, Persepolis and Ecbatana.

It was in Susa that the events recorded in the book of Esther and the vision of Daniel took place (Daniel 8:2). The law code Stele of Hammurabi was discovered at Susa. The site was first excavated by the archaeologist W. K. Loftus in AD 1851 and has since been taken over by the French.

Nehemiah 1:4–11

Weep for the city

When we see things as God sees them then we can share his heart for the situation, and it usually leads to prayer.

The words of Hanani reached right down into Nehemiah's heart and brought him to tears (verse 4). This in turn led to mourning, fasting and deep committed prayer. Then Nehemiah really began to share the father-heart of God for Jerusalem: a feeling which was now sharpening up into a vision of God's will which would drive Nehemiah into action.

Jesus wept over the city of Jerusalem as he shared his Father's heart (Luke 19:41). His grief led to action as first he drove the money-changers out of the temple and ultimately went to his crucifixion. God's love went into action as Jesus died in my place and your place so that we can be rebuilt into the image of God.

It is told how, when Salvation Army workers on the mission-field felt they had come to a dead-end and told the founder, William Booth, he sent back the message, 'Try tears.'

True vision is born only when we share God's heart for a particular situation. True vision comes from being put in the picture to the point that your heart aches for something to be done about it. Developing a real burden for a situation makes you cry out to God and drives you to prayer. Deep, committed, heartfelt prayer leads to the discovery of God's will and purpose – then it is time to act.

Too many people want Jesus to be their Saviour, to free them from their sins, but want to stop there. Real growth with God means catching the vision for his will and purpose and then having the desire to do something about it.

Questions

1. Have you ever wept before God in desperation over something or someone?
2. Why do you think Nehemiah wept, then mourned and fasted?
3. Should the church ask for God's help when it is not prepared to carry it out?

Biblical terms

King's cupbearer (verse 11)
The Hebrew verb used means literally 'to give to drink'. So cupbearer means 'one who gives (someone) something to drink'. The same word occurs in 1 Kings 10:5 and 2 Chronicles 10:5. In some versions it is translated 'butler' (e.g. Genesis 40:1; 41:9). But the word 'butler' comes from an old English word meaning 'bottle attendant', and consequently loses something of the intended meaning here.

It was quite an important position of influence, with direct access to the king. In the Book of Tobit (the Apocrypha) the ruler Esarhaddon's cupbearer was said to be second only to the king (Tobit 1:22). The Greek historian Herodotus records how King Cambyses appointed one of his friends' sons to the position of cupbearer as a great favour.[6]

Nehemiah 2:1–9

The King's commission

Even when it seems impossible, the desire to carry out God's will and to respond to a vision given by him will open doors in most unexpected ways.

Nehemiah held an important position in the king's household so it was unlikely that he would be released to respond to God's call to go to Jerusalem.

Nehemiah writes, 'I was very much afraid' (verse 2). There are probably two reasons for this statement. First, it was a time of festivity (probably a drinking party; cf. verse 1 and Esther 1:3–4) and because Nehemiah looked miserable on such an occasion, he was risking the king's anger. Secondly, he knew that the king had given orders for building work at Jerusalem to be stopped (Ezra 4:8–23). So how was the king going to react to the request Nehemiah was about to put to him? Notice Nehemiah does not actually name Jerusalem (2:5).

If the king felt that Nehemiah was involved in some plot against him, then Nehemiah's life would be at stake. Kings in those days were often quite paranoic, and with good reason. Many were killed by those who were close to them.

Nehemiah needed the king's permission to carry out the King's commission, but how? He never seemed to lose the proper perspective on his situation. When the king asked him what he wanted, Nehemiah's number one priority was prayer (verse 5).

He may well have remembered the task God gave to Moses to go back to Egypt (where Moses was wanted for murder) and ask one of the most powerful rulers of the time to let a large proportion of his slaves (who were carrying out his building programme free of charge) go free. An impossible task, yet the Hebrew nation was released and after forty years in the wilderness made it into the land just as God had promised them. (Most of this story is found in the book of Exodus through to the book of Judges.)

Jesus also dealt with a seemingly impossible situation with his disciples. While he was up the Mount of Transfiguration some of the disciples had tried to help a young boy who was possessed by a spirit. On Jesus' return, when the father asked him if he could help, Jesus' response was, 'If you can? … Everything is possible for him who believes' (Mark 9:23). Then he restored the lad to full health. Afterwards the disciples asked him why they had failed, and Jesus answered, 'This kind can come out only by prayer' (Mark 9:14–29).

Throughout the history of the church those regarded as people of vision have also been people of prayer. They lived by the conviction that the task ahead was nothing compared to the power behind them.

Nehemiah was just about to begin a journey both physically and spiritually. He was only just beginning to experience the power of prayer and what it means to serve the God of the impossible.

Nothing significant has changed; God is still calling people of prayer and vision to rebuild a fallen world and a damaged society. To misquote a former president of the United States, the late J. F. Kennedy, 'Ask not what God can do for you, but rather what you can do for God.' Our calling is to serve the God of the impossible and carry out the King's commission.

Questions

1. Can you think of times in your life when prayer has changed things? How?
2. Does your church believe in miracles?

3. How many times do people say it cannot be done, with the result that nothing happens?

Biblical terms

The queen sitting beside him (verse 6)
This phrase is included for no apparent reason. We know from Persian texts that Artaxerxes' queen was called Damaspia (*Persika* 15:44). However, the queen is not named here and the word translated queen is not the usual one, but a much less popular word usually used of 'a concubine' or 'woman of the harem' (Judges 5:30; Psalms 45:10; Daniel 5:2–3, 23).

Whoever she was, she was important enough for Nehemiah to mention her. Perhaps she may have had a hand in persuading the king to go along with Nehemiah's request.

Personalities

Asaph (verse 8)
He was the warden of the forests to the king. The forests are probably those in Lebanon that had supplied the wood for the building of the temple of Solomon (see the note on Ezra 2:7).

His name is Jewish in origin (which may be why Nehemiah knew him by name).

Nehemiah 2:10–16

Know the worst

**To achieve the best for God it is important
to be realistic and to know the worst
in a situation first.**

It is interesting to observe how Nehemiah went about carrying out the king's
commission once he had arrived in
Jerusalem.

He did not charge straight in with a lot of fuss and com-
motion. He did not instantly proclaim himself as God's
answer to all the troubles of the people of God. Instead he
kept quiet until he had a full grasp of the situation. The
enemy, Sanballat and Tobiah, had already got wind of
Nehemiah's presence and it would not do to face them
unprepared.

Sanballat the Horonite (verse 10) is mentioned not only
in Scripture but also in the *Elephantine Papyri* (letters from
Jews in Elephantine, Egypt). There he is known as the governor of Samaria, and reference is also made to his two
sons. His name, which is Babylonian, means 'the god Sin
has given life'.[7] This is supported by Nehemiah 4:2, where
Sanballat has an army, and 6:2–5, where he summons
Nehemiah as an equal.

In a letter (407BC) to Bagoas, the governor of Judah,[8] his
sons are named as Delaiah and Shemaiah. Both names are
based on the name of God (*Yahweh*), so he may well have
worshipped the God of Israel. One of his daughters was
married to Joiada, son of Eliashib the high priest
(Nehemiah 13:28).

The fact that he is called a Horonite implies that he came
from the town of Horonaim. That could be a place in

Moab (Jeremiah 48:3) or the village of Beth-Horon eighteen miles north-west of Jerusalem. Sanballat was probably the descendant of one of the foreign families who settled there in the eighth century (2 Kings 17:24).

Tobiah (verse 10) has a Hebrew name meaning 'the Lord is good'. He obviously has strong ties with priestly Jewish families (6:17–19; 13:4). The name Tobiah was well known in Moab at the later time of Greek influence. The name is also linked with the Jerusalem priesthood,[9] so it may be that they were descendants of this Tobiah. It is strange, therefore, that he is described as an Ammonite. Unless it means simply that he was the Persian appointed governor of the region because he is of equal status with Sanballat.

Nehemiah realized that he would have to know the worst about the situation before he could begin to work for God's best. There was no point in being so heavenly minded that he was of no earthly use! So, quietly by night, he set out to assess the state of the city walls. Nehemiah, the night-rider, found the walls in such a bad state that he was forced to dismount from his animal, but at least now he could make a realistic evaluation of the task to be achieved. Still he had told no-one (verse 16).

In the context of the Sermon on the Mount, on the subject of service, prayer and fasting (Matthew 6:1–18), Jesus warned about the hypocrites (religious leaders) who liked to shout about their good works. He implies that their only real interest was to blow their own trumpets. When God calls believers to carry out the work of the kingdom, it is not for us to seek personal gratification. Nor should we charge in without knowing the full facts, like a child running full tilt down a hillside out of control. Jesus knew the worst (the cross) but then achieved God's best (victory over sin and death). The message of Nehemiah has not changed – know the worst, then you can work for the best.

Questions

---

1. Do you ever say something and then wish you had thought about it first?
2. Are there situations where the church duplicates work already being done because no-one bothered to ask first?
3. What is the worst and best in God's call on your life?

Geography

Landmarks of the city (verses 13–15)
This is one of the best descriptions of the city of Jerusalem during this period that we have on record. There are some difficulties in working out the exact location of all the places mentioned because the precise line followed by the city walls changed from one period to the next. Some gates named here cannot be found and probably disappeared during King Herod's rebuilding in the city. Interestingly, the archaeologist Kathleen Kenyon, when discussing Nehemiah's description of the city walls, says, 'The archaeological evidence ... fits the literary evidence very well'.[10]

The Valley Gate (verse 13) is said to be about 1,500 yards from the Dung Gate, where the rubbish was removed from the city (still there today), on the western wall. It led to the Tyropeon or Cheesemakers Valley and could well be the Potsherd Gate of Jeremiah 19:2.

The King's pool (verse 14) is probably the 'Pool of Siloam' (3:15, cf. John 9:7) near to the Fountain Gate, a basin fed by the Gihon Spring. It still exists and is known today as *Birket el Hamra*. When she excavated this part of the city Kathleen Kenyon wrote: 'The tumble-down stones uncovered by our trench is a vivid example of the ruinous state of the eastern side of Jerusalem that balked Nehemiah's donkey'.[11]

Nehemiah 2:17–18

One for all and all for one

People working together for the kingdom achieve far more than those who just want to do their own thing.

The foundations for the task had been laid in prayer, fasting and vision. Then came the commission, determination and investigation. Now Nehemiah calls the Jewish people to work together to rebuild the walls of the city. He calls for co-operation to restore the honour of God and informs them of the goodwill of King Artaxerxes towards the task.

The word 'hand', symbolic of power and strength, is used in two different ways in these few verses. First Nehemiah claims God's authority by saying, 'the gracious hand of my God is upon me'. Then the Jews respond by 'making their hands strong for the work' (see the note on verse 18). It could almost be paraphrased as 'Many hands make light work, especially when God is giving a hand.'

Nehemiah could not rebuild on his own; it was important that all the people of God played their part.

A rowing boat needs all hands on the oars. Too many passengers and it gets nowhere fast. Too much one-sided rowing and it goes round in circles. To be fast and effective everyone needs to give a hand.

There is no room for passengers in the work of the kingdom of God. Jesus, using the imagery of harvest-time, remarked to his disciples that the work needs to be done, but the workers are few (Matthew 9:37; Luke 10:2).

The motto of the three musketeers in Alexander Dumas' novel of the same name should also be the motto of the church of Jesus Christ: 'One for all and all for one' if we are to see the kingdom come, God's will done and his name given due honour.

Questions

1. What is the task God is calling you to cooperate in?
2. Can you achieve more on your own or by working with others? Why?
3. Why do some churches insist on doing their own thing regardless of other Christians in the area?

Biblical terms

So they began this good work (verse 18)
It is not entirely clear why the NIV translates the text here in this way. The actual Hebrew text is 'so they made their hands strong for good'. This is a Hebrew phrase meaning that they were encouraged.

The word translated as 'discourage' in Ezra (4:4) literally means 'weakened their hands' and was a well-known idiom of the time. So what we have here in verse 18 is the opposite, that is 'they were encouraged by (his) cooperation', which is different in its emphasis.

Nehemiah 2:19-20

Who is on the Lord's side?

Partnership in God's purposes needs to be clearly defined – it takes only one bad apple to spoil the rest.

Nehemiah had gained the confidence of the people gathered in Jerusalem and now there was an air of real excitement and enthusiasm to begin the work of rebuilding the walls. However, when God is at work with his people then the devil, or his representatives, will usually be on hand to try to make things difficult.

Geshem (verse 19) was the third enemy of Nehemiah to be mentioned by name. He is also called Gashmu (6:6) in some translations. He is described as Geshem the Arab and there is evidence to show that he may well have been from a north Arabian tribe called the Kedarites. They crop up quite frequently in the Old Testament (Genesis 25:13; 1 Chronicles 1:29; Isaiah 21:16–17; 42:11; 60:7; Jeremiah 2:10; 49:28–33; Ezekiel 27:21). By the time of Nehemiah they had settled in the Transjordan area and down to the Nile Delta.

It has been suggested that part of the reason for Geshem's opposition to the new Jewish governor, Nehemiah, was that this strengthened province might interfere with trade. The powerful north Arabian confederacy controlled an area from north-east Egypt to northern Arabia and southern Palestine. It gained much wealth from the myrrh and frankincense business.[12]

A bowl was discovered in 1947 at Tell el-Maskhuata in Egypt with the inscription 'Cain son of Gashmu king of Kedar' on it. This is almost certainly a reference to the same Geshem.

Sanballat, Tobiah and Geshem represented the surrounding nations and they saw this conviction and unity among the Jews as a real threat to their own interests and power; something had to be done to stop it.

The first move was to attempt to lower the morale of the workers and break their spirit before things went too far. Mockery, false accusations and ridicule are the stock-in-trade of opponents of God. Nehemiah's response was immediate; you have no legal, political or religious claim on this work (verse 20).

When Jesus began his public ministry, immediately he was baptized and the Holy Spirit came down, Satan was waiting for him in the wilderness to tempt him away from his work. Jesus consistently countered Satan's remarks with God's word – 'it is written' (Matthew 4:1–11).

Self-interest and a desire for power are often the reasons Christians meet opposition when living out their lives according to God's will. So it is important to face attacks straight away and deal with them in a godly and biblical manner.

If you have a bad apple in a fruit bowl, the longer you leave it there the more fruit it will infect. It is best to take it out immediately and avoid further problems.

If you ignore problems, they do not go away, they just get bigger. When you are under any form of attack, be it ridicule or false accusations, recognize the enemy as well as your allies. Know who is on the Lord's side and act accordingly.

Questions

1. If people laugh at you and say untrue things about you because of your beliefs, how do you handle it?
2. What would your church do if someone came along to your church service and began to heckle the preacher?
3. Where do you draw the line in working in cooperation with people of other faiths or no faith at all?

5

Working together

Nehemiah 3:1 – 6:16

Nehemiah 3:1–32

Equal opportunities

God has a part for everyone to play in his purposes, often those who, in the eyes of the world, do not appear exactly suitable.

Work on the walls begins and this chapter gives us a record of who did what, where and with whom.

The use of language suggests that the north wall was completely destroyed because it had to be rebuilt whereas other parts were simply repaired.

Of the repairs carried out on the walls by the priests, Levites, gatekeepers, tradespeople, women, craftsmen (including goldsmiths and perfume makers) and officials, forty-one separate repairs are listed. The phrase 'next to', which is used again and again in this passage, literally means 'hand by hand'. It repeats the emphasis of 'many hands making light work' in chapter 2.

The northern section had eight task-groups (verses 1–5), the west had ten (verses 6–13), the south had two (verses 14–15) and the east had twenty-one (verses 16–32) because a new wall had to be built here. It was also here that Nehemiah had to dismount from his donkey (verses 2–14).

Shallum's daughters worked alongside the men (verse 12) and a whole town worked together to repair 500 yards of wall (verse 13). But what about the leaders from Tekoa? The people from Tekoa did not get into any arguments, they simply did twice as much work to cover for their leaders (verses 5 and 27).

If I was going to rebuild and restore a city wall, I would probably have called in a professional building company.

Nehemiah, however, called together ordinary people, perfume makers and goldsmiths, men and women alike. What is even more significant is that the work was completed in fifty-two days (6:15) and was good enough to walk on (12:31). The Jews of Jerusalem and the surrounding areas had been called and commissioned and were about to prove they were also capable of carrying out the work.

There is an old hymn which has the line, 'God moves in a mysterious way his wonders to perform', and this is borne out in the account of the repairs to the walls.

If I had been in Jesus' position when he was looking for disciples, I would have gone to Jerusalem Bible College, or the equivalent, for students who came highly recommended by the principal. Jesus went to the north-west of the country and selected Galileans. Galilee was an area known for its strong northern accent and rebellious people. In Jerusalem they were regarded as being 'a bit thick', but they knew they had been with Jesus (Acts 4:13).

It may not make a lot of sense in respect of the world's values but it makes perfect sense in terms of the values of the kingdom of God. Later in history Paul would write to Greek Christians in Corinth who prided themselves on their intellect, 'Not many of you were wise by human standards; not many were influential; not many were of noble birth. But God chose the foolish things of the world to shame the wise; God chose the weak things of the world to shame the strong' (1 Corinthians 1:26–27).

The message of Nehemiah, Jesus and Paul is that God has a special job for each one of us and the main qualification is a willingness to respond to his call. God is a real equal-opportunities employer.

Questions

1. What qualifications do we need to do God's work?
2. What lessons can Christians today learn from the co-operation that took place to achieve God's will?

3. What would you do if some of your leaders refused to
get involved in something that you felt was of God?

Geography

Landmarks of the city (verses 1–32)
The Sheep Gate (verse 1) was built on the eastern part of
the north wall facing the road to Jericho, by the high priest
and his family (see also John 5:2). It could have been the
site of a sheep market much the same as the one held
outside Herod's Gate in the Old City in Jerusalem today.
Some scholars identify it with the Benjamin Gate
(Jeremiah 37:13; 38:7; Zechariah 14:10).

The Fish Gate (verse 3): this may have been the site of a
fish market (Nehemiah 13:16) especially as it was on the
side of the city closest to the sea. Other names in the same
geographical area are the Ephraim Gate (8:16; 12:39; 2
Kings 14:13) and the Middle Gate (Jeremiah 39:3).

The Broad Wall (verse 8) lay between the Ephraim Gate
and the Tower of Ovens (12:38–29). The possibility is that
it was a wall intended to cross the dip between the City of
David and the Temple Mount because it branches off from
the main wall and joins it again by the Pool of Siloam.

In 1970 N. Avigad rediscovered 440 metres of this wall
while excavating the Jewish quarter of the city. It was
found to be seven metres thick.

The Tower of Ovens (verse 11) is likely to have been the
bakers' ovens. They were located south of the Broad Wall
(12:38). Jeremiah speaks of the Bakers' Street that may be
connected (Jeremiah 37:21).

The City of David is used here to mean a smaller part of
Jerusalem. It was on the south-eastern hill of the main city
and to the north west of the Gihon Spring. It was the original Jebusite town that David captured, sometimes called
Zion (2 Samuel 5:7), and covered an area of about fifteen
acres. The city had the Tyropeon valley to its western side,

the Hinnom valley to the south, and the Kidron valley to the east. Solomon enlarged it to the north taking in the temple mound (1 Kings 3:1; 11:27).

Nehemiah 4:1-3

Angry opposition

The people of God can expect opposition from others when they carry out God's will – mockery is a favourite method of the ungodly, followed by anger.

Sanballat had tried to prevent the work from starting and had failed. Now the work was in progress it was no longer an idea to be laughed at – there was a real possibility, even probability, that the wall would be reconstructed. Sanballat was angry! The Hebrew word used implies 'being heated' or 'on fire'. As is often the case, he had his cronies with him, as well as the army of Samaria. The threat to Nehemiah had moved from words to a real physical threat in this show of force.

Sanballat questions the ability of the Jews to rebuild the walls but, despite mocking them in front of his friends and allies, he was obviously taking them seriously. Tobiah adds fuel to the fire when he implies the wall would not even hold the weight of a fox walking on it (verse 3). According to Oscar Wilde, 'Sarcasm is the lowest form of wit and the highest form of ignorance.' It certainly did not stop the work from continuing.

It is rare for the work of God's people to go unopposed. If you love God it is highly likely that those who do not share your convictions will not love you (John 15:19–21).

Jesus was and is the most perfect person who has ever

lived and even he had his critics. He was subjected to taunts and physical threats similar to those faced by Nehemiah and yet he was not defeated. Despite everything the opposition could throw at him, Jesus completed the work his father sent him to do with the cry, 'It is finished' (John 19:30).

It should come to us as no surprise when we meet the same kind of reaction. Jesus warned his disciples that opposition and persecution would come and offered hope through perseverance: 'Blessed are you when people insult you, persecute you and falsely say all kinds of evil against you because of me' (Matthew 5:11).

Questions

1. How do you feel and react when you are criticized?
2. Do you know of people who have been threatened physically because they are Christians?
3. What do you think Jesus meant when he said we are blessed when we are persecuted for him?

Nehemiah 4:4–6

Prayer changes things

Sometimes we pray when under pressure because we rdesire evenge, but retribution is for God to decide, not us.

Nehemiah always turns to prayer in crucial situations and this one was no exception. The prayer seems a harsh one when we read it today in a different cultural setting. Why did Nehemiah pray in the way that he did?

Psalm 137 (made famous by the singing group 'Boney M') begins by expressing the feeling of being isolated and a long way from home. The content of the psalm moves from sadness to anger at being in captivity. It ends with a prayer of bitterness asking God to smash against the rocks the heads of the babies of their enemies. Hardly a prayer of love and compassion!

Similar prayers can be found in Psalm 7, 35, 58, 59, 69, 83, 109, 137, 139. They appear more than a little uncharitable to us today. However, Nehamiah knew this was God's work and so those who were opposing him were against God. It is not a personal desire for punishment, which is put into God's hands. The covenant of Abraham included curses on the enemies of Israel (Genesis 12:1–3) and supports Nehemiah's concern that no-one should sneer at the work of God.

Having 'got it out of his system', Nehemiah returns to the task in hand, rebuilding the wall. He has the same kind of determination that Jesus reflected when he commented, 'Destroy this temple, and I will raise it again in three days' (John 2:19).

There are occasions when we can feel so frustrated by evil actions that we are tempted to take the law into our own hands. However, it is for God to act as judge, not you or me and this is clearly stated in Deuteronomy 32:35 (quoted in Romans 12:19 and Hebrews 10:30).

Human nature seems to have an in-built desire to want to have a say in what goes on, to act as judge and jury on the lives of others. Peter, for example, wanted to know what Jesus had to say about John and was told in so many words, by Jesus, to mind his own business (John 21:23). Minding my own business means getting on with the job God has called me to do. The only way I am free to comment on other people's lives is in prayer.

Like Nehemiah, it is our responsibility to take it to the Lord in prayer, knowing that it is prayer that ultimately changes things. Then it is back to work.

Questions

1. Can you pray for Satan to be saved?
2. Jesus says to love your enemies (Matthew 5:44), but is that easier said than done? How can we love our enemies?
3. Does your church pray about people they do not like, or who make them angry and upset?

Nehemiah 4:7–9

Watch and pray

Prayer is one aspect of spiritual warfare, another is being constantly ready for attacks.

They were surrounded: to the west were the men of Ashdod; to the north were Samaritans led by Sanballat; to the east were Tobiah and the Ammonites; and to the south were the Arabs, including the Edomites, led by Geshem. It was rather like the feeling the Jews have in Israel today! It also gives some insight into the problems of a central government trying to maintain order from a distance. Persia was a long way away. (See the map on page 22).

The leaders of the surrounding areas continued to do everything they could to prevent the work being completed. Nehemiah's strategy against them followed similar lines to that of Jesus when he said, 'Watch and pray' (Matthew 26:41; Mark 14:38; Luke 21:36), emphasizing the necessity of being constantly on guard against attack.

There is a story told of the evangelist Dwight L. Moody coming by ship to conduct a mission in Britain. One of his followers informed him that the ship was on fire and enquired as to whether they should pray about it. 'Ay lad, as we're passing the fire buckets', came the reply.

The kingdom of God is a partnership between God and his people, each playing a responsible part. God helps those who help themselves and the call is consistently the same. Be practical in your spirituality, constantly before God in prayer and at the same time ready for anything. Watch and pray.

Questions

1. Is it reasonable to expect God to help us when we are not prepared to do anything ourselves?
2. What kind of attacks does your church have to be on guard against?
3. Who do you think are the enemies of the church?

Biblical terms

The repairs (verse 7)
The Hebrew word used here is not the word generally used for 'repair' in Nehemiah. Taken literally the word means 'the healing (of an injury)' or 'health', 'recovery', 'restoration' (Jeremiah 8:22; 30:17; 33:6).

The more usual word for 'repair' means 'to grow firm or strong' (Nehemiah 3:4–12, 16–18, 22–23, 28–32).

Nehemiah 4:10-14

Fight for the family

To fight for those you love and care about the most is one of the greatest incentives to overcome fear and doubt in the face of the enemy.

With the amount of opposition they were facing and the size of the task still to be completed the people began to be discouraged. In much the same way as the black slaves on the American cotton plantations sang of their troubles, so the labourers began to sing (verse 10). The word 'said' is used not 'sing', but this part of the passage is written in a poetic style. It appears from the style of writing that the people were singing in the form of a lament. It had a rhythm of three beats followed by two that was a common style of the time. They were probably singing it as they worked, not the most encouraging words to work on!

It's hard to get an exact feel of the Hebrew but the following is a suggestion.

> The strength of the labourers is giving out.
> There is so much rubble
> That on our own
> We cannot rebuild the walls.
> Our enemies said 'Before they hear or see us
> We will be there among them
> We will kill them
> And put an end to the work.'

Singing has been a way of expressing strong feelings and coping with life for a long time. The psalms cover just about every emotion from frustration to great joy. Modern spirituals follow in this tradition, having evolved from the songs of the black slaves. 'Nobody know the trouble I've seen, nobody knows but Jesus' is a well-known example.

Nehemiah revealed his skills as a leader when he posted people on the walls in family groups (verse 13). Then he pointed out to them that God was on their side and it was their responsibility to fight for their families (verse 14).

Over the centuries no other institution has survived the changes, pains and pressures of life so consistently as the family. When God created Adam he said that it was not good for man to be alone and so the first family began (Genesis 2:18). When God spoke to Abraham he promised him he would be the father of many nations. Israel developed as a nation out of a family of twelve brothers. A number of the Ten Commandments are concerned with the protection of the family, such as honouring your father and mother and not committing adultery (Exodus 20:12, 14).

Love for family will keep people pressing on when all else fails and Nehemiah recognized the fact. Jesus faced the cross because of his love for the Father and the family of man. We become his relatives, brothers and sisters, when we accept him and his sacrifice for us (John 1:12). The church is the family of God's people and worth fighting for against all comers. Fight for the family!

Questions

1. What songs come to your mind when you find life a struggle?
2. What weapons do you think God wants us to use in fighting for good?
3. How would you feel about giving your life for a member of your family?

History

Swords, spears, bows (verse 13)

The sword is the most frequently mentioned weapon in the Bible and is often used as a symbol for the Word of God (Ezekiel 21:9; Ephesians 6:17). It was seen as the main offensive weapon of war (Isaiah 51:19; Jeremiah 14:15; 24:10; Ezekiel 7:15; 33:6).

The spear had a wooden shaft and a metal head – iron by this time – and was the main weapon of foot soldiers.

Bows were made of animal horn with strips of wood to make up the frame and were strung with sinew or gut. As a weapon it came into general use in Israel when chariots came onto the scene because this required long-range weaponry. The archers from the tribe of Benjamin were quite famous for their skills (1 Chronicles 8:40; 12:2; 2 Chronicles 14:8; 17:17).

Nehemiah 4:15–23

Swords and shovels

Doing God's will means faith and works – there has to be a balance between being warriors and workers.

No peace for the wicked or the godly either! It would be relatively easy to organize the people in Jerusalem into an army to guard the city, but then no work would be done. On the other hand, they could get on with the work but be exposed to constant attack.

Nehemiah had the answer – swords and shovels! Half the task-force went on guard while the other half worked on the walls. Even the workers worked with one hand while they retained a sword in the other; from first thing in the morning until last thing at night.

If there was an attack on another section of the wall, the trumpet would sound and everyone would rally to the place of need, knowing it might be them next time. So they could be constantly at the ready everyone kept their clothes on at night – that way they wouldn't be caught 'napping', so to speak.

The phrase 'the man who sounded the trumpet' (verses 18–20) is translated from the Hebrew for 'ram's horn'. As well as being used in worship trumpets were used to sound a warning. The trumpeter had a key role to play in times of war (Judges 3:27; 6:34; 7:18; 1 Samuel 13:3; 2 Samuel 20:1). The historian Josephus tells us that Nehemiah had trumpeters placed every 500 feet along the wall.[13]

Trumpeters gave the signal to break camp and to retreat from battle. The priest Phineas used one in Israel's battle with Midian (Numbers 31:6) and priests again sounded the trumpets in the war between Abijah and Jeroboam (2 Chronicles 13:12–15). When the battle began the trumpet was sounded to signal the people to give the battle cry (Joshua 6:5–6; Judges 7:16–17). The trumpet was sounded again to announce the end of hostilities (2 Samuel 18:16; 20:22). When you could no longer hear the trumpet it was a sign of peace in Hebrew culture (Jeremiah 42:14).

When Paul talks about putting on the armour of God (Ephesians 6:10–20), the armour he mentions is all for guarding the front of the body and is a reminder of how much we need to protect each other when we are vulnerable. We all need each other. Once it is put on, Paul does not seem to suggest it should be taken off: like Nehemiah's builders, the Christian needs to be always at the ready.

The other issue which is highlighted here is the

importance of getting on with the work God has called us to do. James said that 'faith without deeds is dead' (James 2:14–26). Christianity is not faith or action but faith in action; that is, swords and shovels.

Questions

1. What do you think is the equivalent of a sword and shovel for the Christian today?
2. How can you and I be ready at all times, on guard against the attacks of Satan?
3. What examples can you think of which illustrate faith in action in the church?

Nehemiah 5:1–5

The cry of the poor

Good news for the widow, the orphan and the stranger is a condition of restoration. In the same way that you show love for the least, you show your love for God.

Poverty was a big problem. The farmers were not able to look after their fields because of the wall building, so they did not have time to grow enough food to live on. Also, trade would be bad because of hostilities with the surrounding nations.

There were three further reasons for poverty in Jerusalem at this time. People deliberately had large families as an insurance for old age; when there was no social security system you had to depend even more on the family. Secondly, when times were hard and there were no financial reserves, it was a case of going into debt to buy food or starving. Thirdly, the Persian kings levied a tax on land, known as the king's tax, which everyone had to pay whether they could afford to or not.

In addition, the rich were taking advantage of the poor in their need (verse 5). They were from the same tribes, working together to restore Jerusalem. So it is not really surprising that the poor began to complain, especially when they were forced to sell members of their family into slavery. 'A great outcry against their Jewish brothers' (verse 1) is the phrase used. This phrase has legal overtones (Genesis 18:20–21; Exodus 12:30; Job 34:28). The outcry arose out of an imbalance of resources between the common people and those referred to here as 'the Jews'. Although the NIV adds the word 'brothers' (cf. verse 5) to help clarify the relationship.

The phrase 'the Jews' seems to have some technical meaning (2:16; 5:17) which makes it distinct and separate from the ordinary people. The use may imply some form of middle-class culture within the Hebrew nation.

Jesus expressed his own deep concern about justice for the poor in stories like the Great Banquet, the Sheep and the Goats (Matthew 25:31–46), and his reading of the Isaiah passage in Luke 4. There has to be good news for the poor if there is to be good news at all.

The same issue has been raised many times throughout the history of the church. Self-interest amongst Christians has persistently maintained situations of injustice, not only in the world, but amongst God's people! It brought about tension between slaves and their masters in the early church. It also raised serious questions regarding pay and conditions in the last century in Britain, for example between the owners of coal mines, cotton mills and factories and their workers, especially as many worshipped in the same churches. Some Lancashire mill owners would not hire people who did not, or would not, attend their chapels.

The Bible is consistent in its teaching on this issue; those people of God who 'have' are responsible for helping those who 'have not'. People of the Bible such as Amos and James express quite clearly God's concern when the religious rich exploit the godly poor (Amos 5:11–15; James 5:1–6).

God is a God of love, but he is also a God of justice and calls his people to reflect that in their own lives. Only then can we expect the kingdom on earth as it is in heaven. As Mahatma Ghandi said 'There is enough for the world's need but not the world's greed.'

Questions

1. Who are the widows, orphans and strangers in our society? How can we help them?
2. Why is the church in the West essentially middle-class in culture? For example, council-estate churches are usually very small, if they exist at all.
3. How do you think we as Christians could do more to consider the needs of others instead of making sure we are comfortable?

Biblical terms

The men and their wives (verse 1)
The word 'men' would be better translated 'common people'. The most common use of the Hebrew word is 'people' or 'nation' (Nehemiah 1:8; 9:22) and the translation into 'men' is misleading.

'And their wives' has an unusual emphasis because in the Jewish culture of this period women would not normally be expected to speak, but things were so difficult that even they cried out.

History

Mortgaging (verse 3)

Borrowing by pledging (property and/or family members) was a common practice of the poor in order to buy food or to pay taxes (2 Kings 4:1–2).

The law on this procedure was carefully balanced to ensure that there should be no long-term hardship as a result. Seven years was the maximum time in slavery for debt (Exodus 21:2–11; Deuteronomy 15:12–18), then the person was to be released. A similar law applied to property (Leviticus 25:10–33; Ezekiel 18:7). It should be noted that 'daughters' are mentioned specifically in verse 4 because they were particularly at risk. They could be made to marry the owner or one of his sons and this would make it next to impossible for them to gain their freedom (cf. Exodus 21:7–11). The word 'mortgage' is only used in this sense in this verse of Nehemiah.

The basic problem was the age-old one; people will ignore the law if they can get away with it and there is financial advantage in doing so.

The king's tax (verse 4)

This was a land tax according to the amount of land held. In the position of governor, Nehemiah would be responsible for collecting it and paying it to the king (after deducting his own expenses).

This form of taxation led to an accumulation of wealth for the already wealthy and increased debt and hardship for the poor. Documents from Babylon show that many were unable to redeem their property and were forced to sell their children into slavery. Many poor people escaped to the big cities to avoid having to pay their debts.[14]

Nehemiah 5:6–13

Justice for all

If there is no justice for all then there is no justice at all.

Not only were the wealthy taking the poor into slavery, they were selling them to foreigners (verse 8). This form of oppression made it much harder for them to be bought back. It also gave the other nations the opportunity to have a laugh at Israel's expense.

Nehemiah, like God, heard the cry of the poor in Jerusalem and pointed out the injustice of the behaviour of the wealthy. You can sense his frustration when he points out that as fast as he and his friends were buying the poor out of slavery, others in positions of power were forcing the poor back into servitude (verse 8).

Nehemiah called for a cancellation of all debts and received a very positive response – everyone said, 'Amen', and did as they had promised (verse 13).

Jesus tells a parable which reflects Nehemiah's sentiments. He tells of a man who had a great debt cancelled but then went on to have a man imprisoned for being unable to repay him a much smaller amount (Matthew 18:23–35). Jesus was speaking of forgiveness at the time and it is an important reminder to each one of us that God has cancelled our debts because Jesus paid the price on the cross. The call is to forgive others as God has forgiven us.

It is not helpful for the poor to be lectured on why they are in a mess. That is rather like Aesop's fable of the drowning man. While the man is drowning someone leans over the water's edge and says to him, 'You really should have learned to swim before you went in there!'

Nehemiah calls on the people to 'walk in the fear of God' (verse 9) to avoid giving the enemy an opportunity to take advantage.

Questions

1. Do you think Christians should help the poor if their poverty is a result of their own bad management of money? How?
2. What do you think is the difference between a human sense of justice and God's justice?
3. 'Why should I share what I have with other people, after all I have worked hard for it?' How would you respond to someone in your church who said that to you?

History

Usury (verse 7)

The lending of money and charging of interest have always been legal. However, what was not allowed under Jewish law was attempting to make a profit out of a fellow Jew's poverty and distress. According to the law, no interest was to be charged if the loan was made to someone undergoing hard times (Exodus 22:35; Leviticus 25:35–38; Deuteronomy 15:7–8; 23:19).

Biblical terms

We have bought back (verse 8)

In Jewish law it was the responsibility of the nearest blood relative or kinsman to act as 'redeemer', that is, to buy back property or family members sold in hard times.

One of the most well-known accounts of this is in the

129

book of Ruth, where Boaz assumes the responsibilities of kinsman and brings Ruth out of poverty back into a family (Ruth 3:9, 12; 4:1, 3, 6, 8, 14). Here Nehemiah takes on the role of the redeemer. Both Jeremiah and Isaiah portray God as the redeemer or kinsman of his people (Isaiah 41:14; 43:14; 44:6, 24; 47:4; 48:17; 49:7, 26; 54:5, 8; 59:20; 63:16; Jeremiah 50:34).

Jesus becomes the ultimate redeemer as he takes on the role of the nearest kinsman to the whole world. He has bought the world back from sin by his own blood (Luke 24:21; Galatians 3:13–14; 1 Peter 1:18; Revelation 5:9).

Shook out the folds (verse 13)
In those times people kept personal belongings and money in a pocket in the folds of their outer garments. By shaking the folds to show he had nothing left, Nehemiah made a significant statement to all who ignored his call to help the poor. They would have nothing left and neither God nor his people would be their blood relations.

Nehemiah 5:14–19

Practise what you preach

**People are more convinced by what is said
if they also see those who say it putting it into action
in their own lives.**

Nehemiah puts what he preaches into action by not claiming the governor's food allowance (verses 14, 18). The governor of an area had the right to deduct from taxes collected for the king his own living allowance and expenses and those of his household. Because of the hardships on the people Nehemiah did not claim his entitlement (compare with Solomon: 1 Kings 4:22–23).

Nehemiah could have exercised his right as governor to collect his salary from the taxes (1 Corinthians 9:8–15) but, like any good leader, he led by example and denied himself the right in order to avoid imposing further suffering on the poor. Wherever he got his money from it was not through taxation, even though he had to feed an extra 150 people 'at my table' (verse 17). It was considered a privilege to eat at the table of the king or some high official, like eating at the captain's table on board ship, and it was a common practice for the ruler (for example 2 Samuel 9:7, 13; 19:29, 34; 1 Kings 10:5; 18:19; Daniel 1:5–15). Jesus tells a parable on the subject (Luke 14:7–14; compare with Luke 22:27–30).

This account of Nehmiah's conduct is taken from a personal diary and not from a public proclamation. He seems to have worked not only on the basis of 'do what I say', but 'follow my example' also. He did not shout from the rooftops about his behaviour, neither buying up land, nor claiming entertainment expenses: his only concern was what God thought about his conduct (verse 19).

I have been in many places where items of furniture have plaques on them proclaiming the giver. Sometimes phrases like 'To the glory of God' are used, but normally such words are in smaller lettering than the name of the person who made the donation. Surely if we practise what we preach then we should be concerned to see God's name in large letters and not so anxious to gain approval for ourselves?

People are much more convinced of the effect Jesus has had on our lives by our actions than by our words. When Peter and John put their faith into practice before the Jewish high council, the Sanhedrin, their behaviour led others to the conclusion that they had been with Jesus (Acts 4:13). It is not a case of words *or* actions but words *and* actions. Practise what you preach.

Questions

1. Which is most important to you, to have the approval of others or God's approval? Why?
2. Have people asked you about your faith because of your actions?
3. What makes the church different from everybody else?

Biblical terms

A hundred and fifty Jews and officials (verse 17)
A stricter translation of this text is 'one hundred and fifty men', so there may well have been women and children present. This would explain the amount of food supplied daily (verse 18) – enough to feed 500 people some scholars suggest.

Nehemiah 6:1–14

Intimidation

In seeking to follow God's way, there are three main traps to avoid: pressure from people around us to see things their way, the call to compromise, and time-wasting.

Three plots of varying subtlety were tried in order to trap Nehemiah. The first was to try to lure him away from Jerusalem (verse 2). The second was to accuse him of rebellion against the Persian Empire (verse 6) and the third was to get him to sin by entering the area of the temple where only a priest could go: for everyone else it could invoke the death penalty (verse 10; see Numbers 1:51; 3:10; 18:7).

The open gates were the enemies' last chance of really being able to get at Nehemiah's people. Once the gates were completed (Nehemiah 7:1) it would be much harder to carry out an effective attack. There is a touch of sarcasm in Nehemiah's response that if he responds the work will suffer (verse 3), when that is exactly what the opposition were trying to achieve.

Shemaiah was hired to trick Nehemiah, as a layman, into entering the temple. It is not clear who Shemaiah was (verse 10), nor his actual job or position, though he is descibed as a false prophet and we are given details of his family.

Why Shemaiah was housebound is a puzzle. Had he committed some sin that restricted his movements? Was he carrying out a form of prophetic symbolism: 'As I am housebound, so should Nehemiah be shut in the temple'? Or was he disabled in some way through illness? We can only guess. His prophecy is given in a poetic style that was popular at the time. However, it did not fool Nehemiah, who sidestepped the trap and followed up with a prayer against intimidation (verse 14).

If the devil cannot get you to do anything else, he will try to waste your time in unimportant activities. Rumour and gossip conveying false information have also worked well in bringing the church into disrepute. Notice how quickly the media pick up scandal involving Christians and how slow they are to report good news. It is also important to know where to draw the line in our behaviour as Christians before we go too far. Intimidation can make me drink more than I should, say more than I should and react in a way that I should not. James gives very good practical advice, 'Resist the devil, and he will flee from you. Come near to God and he will come near to you' (James 4:7–8).

Questions

1. Have you experienced pressure from non-Christian friends to do something you know you should not do? If so, how did you handle it?
2. When is temptation hardest to resist in your life?
3. How should the church decide where to draw the line between what is right and wrong?

History

An unsealed letter (verse 5)
This was a piece of papyrus or pottery with no seal on it. Anyone who came in contact with it could read it, and Sanballat intended Nehemiah to know that when he received it. In other words it was a thinly veiled threat.

Nehemiah 6:15–16

It is finished!

Even the most formidable of tasks, undertaken in the most difficult of circumstances, can be achieved with God's help.

Within six months of hearing of the sad state of Jerusalem, Nehemiah had responded to the call and completed the task. At this time the wall was about 2,600 metres in circumference, unless the western hill was included, in which case it was nearer 4,100 metres.[15]

The wall was completed in just fifty-two days by perfume-makers, goldsmiths, priests and women, all working under the firm conviction that God was on their side. Josephus the historian claims the wall took two years and four months to finish.[16] It must be said, however, that he probably guessed this because the wall of Jerusalem was larger in his own time. Fifty-two days seems a reasonable time in which to complete a wall of that size, bearing in mind that much of it was repaired rather than built from scratch. (Josephus made more than a few mistakes over dates: for example, he put Nehemiah in the reign of Xerxes.)

The word 'completed' (verse 15) is from the same root as the word *shalom* and literally means 'to be at peace', or 'to be whole'. Usually it is translated, 'to be restored', 'finished', 'completed'.

The word is used in the same sense when Solomon completed the building of the temple (2 Chronicles 5:1) and to describe the foundations of the temple (Ezra 5:16). It is used only on one other occasion when God speaks of finishing a king's reign (Daniel 5:26).

The knock-on effect of the completion of the wall was that Nehemiah's enemies realized they had lost their battle with him because God was on his side (verse 16).

Jesus reflects the same sense of completing the task in his prayer to the Father (John 17:4) and when he finally triumphs over death on the cross, his cry is, 'It is finished!' (John 19:30).

The hallmark of Christians over the centuries has been that when God is on their side anything is possible. The writer Rudyard Kipling once wrote that for him there was only one thing more frightening than a charge of Dervishes under the leadership of young cavalry officers, and that was a group of Presbyterians rising from their knees after prayer convinced they are about to do the will of the Lord!

After years of hard slog William Wilberforce heard on his death-bed that the slave-trade had been abolished and his task was completed. Gladys Aylward was turned down for missionary work but she went anyway, convinced that God had called her even if others did not recognize it. Martin Luther King gave his life for a vision from God of a day when everyone would be treated equally. Others, inspired by his example carry on the struggle.

We are all called to proclaim the good news of Jesus Christ, regardless of background and ability, and there can be no rest until we too can say 'It is finished!'

Questions

1. What is your response to the phrase, 'When the going gets tough, the tough get going'?
2. When you face an impossible task how do you react?
3. Can you think of something your church has achieved against impossible odds? If so, what was the reaction of others in the community when it was accomplished?

The household of faith

Nehemiah 6:17 – 10:40

Nehemiah 6:17-19

Blood is thicker than water

Close family ties can, and often do, pull people away from practising the godly life and loyalty to God.

As we have already noted in chapter 4, family loyalty and support are normally very strong. In the previous situation Nehemiah had used this to encourage the people to carry on at a time when morale was low. Now the fact that 'blood is thicker than water' was causing Nehemiah a problem. Letters and information were being passed on to the opposition, Tobiah in particular, largely because of family ties (verses 17–18).

Arah (verse 18) is mentioned in Ezra 2:5 and Nehemiah 7:10. It appears that Shemaiah, the son of Shecaniah, the son of Arah, was the guard on the East Gate (Nehemiah 3:29). His sister married Tobiah and their son Jehohanan married the daughter of Meshullam. Meshullam was the son of Berekiah whom we find was the son of Meshezabel. He worked on the section of the wall next to the Fish Gate (Nehemiah 3:4).

With these family ties it was clear why some Jewish nobility kept in close contact with Nehemiah's enemies (see also Nehemiah 13:28). Close friends and family enticing people away from God is a persistent problem – there is a whole section on it in Deuteronomy 13:6–11 where it is considered serious enough to warrant the death penalty.

It was the blood ties between Barnabas and his nephew, John Mark, which led to a disagreement with Paul and caused their splitting up (Acts 15:36–41). Jonathan overcame his family ties in order to ensure fair play for the future King David (1 Samuel 20:1–4).

The same conflicts of interest still arise amongst Christians. Usually it is because a Christian is married to a non-believer. It can also be a problem when a family member who is not a Christian forces the believer to choose between what they want and God's will.

Jesus warned this would happen and calls on people to choose where their commitment lies: family or faith (Matthew 10:34–39).

Questions

1. Have you been asked by a close family member to choose between them and God? What was your response?
2. Do you feel family should come first? If not, why?
3. Can you think of instances where family loyalties within the church have got in the way of the will of God?

Nehemiah 7:1–3

Shut that door!

A wall is only as strong as its weakest point. A chain is only as strong as its weakest link. God's people are effective only when they guard each other's weak spots.

Nehemiah placed his brother in charge of the city because he was family, but justifies his action by commending him as a godly man (verse 2). The NIV adds 'and Hananiah', to the verse, although it offers the alternative 'or Hanani, that is' as a footnote. It is unlikely that

Nehemiah would have appointed two men, especially as their names are variations of the same name – the one is a longer form of the other.

'And' is translated as 'namely' in Ezra 8:18: 'the son of Israel, namely Sherebiah'(RSV). So I suggest it should be read in the same way here in Nehemiah 'my brother, namely Hanani or Hananiah … charge over Jerusalem'. It also makes sense of why Nehemiah had to comment on his brother's faithfulness and God-fearing nature, to avoid being accused of family favouritism.

Now that the gates were in place, it was important to guard them. The city-wall gatekeepers mentioned here (verse 3) have a different task to the temple gatekeepers (verse 45). A full description of their duties is given in 1 Chronicles 9:17–27.

It was no use having good solid walls if the gates were not guarded, and it required godly people to ensure the city was safe. Jesus uses similar imagery when speaking of the good shepherd who guards the gate to the sheep (John 10:7–9).

We all need people we can rely on: the climber depends on the person holding the rope; passengers depend on the driver of a vehicle and Christians on the rest of their fellow-believers, especially those in positions of responsibility.

If there is an area of weakness, it should be dealt with. On the subject of temptation, Paul in his letter to the Galatians talks of being on watch and how to deal with open doors to sin. He says, 'if someone is caught in a sin, you who are spiritual should restore him gently. But watch yourself, or you also may be tempted' (Galatians 6:1). Shut that door!

Questions

1. Who should respond to issues of weakness in the church and how?
2. What do you do to safeguard your own life against temptation?

3. How do you think God protects us against attack from our enemies?

Nehemiah 7:4–72

Family trees

Can you prove you belong?

The walls were rebuilt, the gates were in place and now the houses needed to be repaired ready for people to reoccupy the city. Then Nehemiah found the family trees of those who had come back first from captivity in Babylon (verse 5).

Ten groups of people are mentioned, starting with the leaders who came back with Zerubbabel in the first return. Twelve men are named (verse 7), possibly to represent the twelve tribes as separate entities, although the ten tribes of the northern kingdom, captured in 722BC, seem to have disappeared or been assimilated by this period.

Next in the list come the families or clans. This includes the numbers of each family who had returned. They are identified by where they originally came from.

The next group is a 'who's who' (including those who could not prove their ancestry; verses 61–65), providing a 'who does what' list of those who served in the temple (verses 39–60).

Animals are also mentioned because they measure not only wealth but also will provide food for the people (verses 68–69).

This list is almost identical to the one in Ezra 2:1–70, with one or two variations. The significance of it is not found in the differences, but in where the list occurs in each man's account. Nehemiah's first concern was to rebuild the wall and he records this first; whereas for Ezra a list of those who have already returned to Jerusalem has priority in his account. Now the wall has been completed and it is time to set about rebuilding the people of God.

Family trees are frequent right through the Bible; even Jesus' family tree is included (Matthew 1; Luke 3). Most of us tend to skip them as we find them dull and uninteresting, but what if it was your family tree, a list of all your ancestors?

Many people today go to a lot of time and expense to discover who their ancestors were and where their roots are. They feel the need to prove where they belong. When we accept the sacrifice of Jesus personally and allow him to take control of our lives, we become family with him. How do we prove we belong? Jesus said, 'by their fruit you will recognize them' (Matthew 7:20) when warning those who would claim to belong to him. So what is the fruit which tells you someone is a Christian, a member of the family of Jesus? Paul gives a list in Galatians 5:22–23.

Questions

1. If you had to prove you are a child of God in order to get into heaven, how would you do it?
2. Who are you related to in the kingdom of God and how can you prove it?
3. How does your church decide who can be a member?

Nehemiah 8:1–3

Hear the Word!

Listen and take time to understand God's Word.

 The people had returned to the land of Israel, they had restored the temple to its former glory and rebuilt the city walls. Now it was time to rebuild the people of God.

The people gathered 'as one man' (verse 1) as Ezra the scribe brought God's written word for them to hear. The phrase is used a number of times when referring to calling the nation together for important occasions (Judges 20:1, 8, 11; 1 Samuel 11:7; Ezra 3:1). Solidarity is seen as vital both for identity and action. This finds something of an echo in the prayer of Jesus 'that all of them may be one, Father, just as you are in me and I am in you. May they also be in us so that the world may believe that you have sent me' (John 17:21).

The phrase 'able to understand' (verse 2) is the Hebrew for 'to hear'. Used here it means literally 'all that could hear with understanding'. It is an interesting word because there is no Hebrew word for 'obey'. The implication is that if you hear, then you should obey. Like the mother who implies the same when she shouts at a disobedient child: 'Didn't you hear me?' (Nehemiah 9:29).

A significant part of rebuilding the nation was to hear God's word with the implied emphasis on obeying it. What is worth noting is that they listened attentively (verse 3) from daybreak until noon. These days people sometimes complain when preachers talk for more than fifteen minutes!

Times have changed and so have cultures and customs,

143

but there is a clear statement in Isaiah that 'the word of God stands for ever' (Isaiah 40:8). Jesus compares everyone who heard his words with either a wise or a foolish builder. The wise one built on a solid foundation and survived the storms, the foolish builder ignored him and built on sand, and what he built fell down (Matthew 7:24). If Christians today want to build their lives on solid rock then, amid all the changes, one challenge is still the same: hear the word of the Lord – to hear is to obey.

Questions

1. Do you believe all the Bible as we have it is God's Word?
2. How much time do you take to listen to what God is saying into your life?
3. If God's Word should be obeyed, why do so many in the church ignore it?

Nehemiah 8:4–8

Making sense

When you understand God's Word, it requires a response.

The reading of the Law was done from a wooden platform (verse 4). Literally 'a wooden tower', it must have been fairly large to hold thirteen men. With the wall and the gate behind it acting as a sounding board, the acoustics would probably be quite good. What we have here may be the forerunner of the pulpit, but the word 'tower' gives us more of a clue to its symbolism.

Towers were used to keep watch from, and to give warning to others. There was often a tower in a vineyard to protect it from unwelcome guests (Isaiah 27:3; Israel was seen as God's vineyard). Ezekiel spoke of the role of the watchman in the tower (Ezekiel 3:17; 33:2, 6–7).

Reading the Law to the people was like reminding someone of their wedding vows. They are more than just words; they are a reminder of the depth of relationship and *commitment* between two people. So when we hear and understand God's Word, it reminds us that we too are in a covenant relationship with him: to love, honour and obey.

Questions

1. Why do people read the Bible?
2. How does it affect you when something suddenly becomes clear to you?
3. Using the analogy of marriage, why do Christians break their promises to God when he keeps his to them?

Biblical terms

Positions in worship (verses 5–7)
As Ezra opened the book (in reality he would have unrolled a scroll), the people *stood* (verse 5) and they remained standing (verse 7) for about five to six hours. Standing was something that was done in the presence of a king (Daniel 1:19: compare with Deuteronomy 29:10; 2 Chronicles 18:18). The NIV translates Daniel 1:19 'the king's service', but it is literally 'standing before the king' (see the Authorized Version for example).

They responded with their *arms lifted up* (verse 6). This was a classic Hebrew position for prayer (Exodus 9:29, 33; 17:11; 1 Kings 8:54; 2 Chronicles 6:12–13; Ezra 9:5; Psalms

28:2; 44:20; 63:4; 88:9; 134:2; 141:2; 143:6; Isaiah 1:15). Psalm 119:48 is a specific response to the Law of God, and Lamentations 1:17 may give some clue to the origin of the position in begging or pleading.

Then in verse 6 they *bowed down* and prostrated themselves, *faces to the ground* (see note on Ezra 9:5).

The leaders 'instructed the people in the law while the people were standing there' (verse 7).

Nehemiah 8:9–12

Don't be sad

The joy of the Lord is your strength.

The people were gathered together to celebrate the Feast of Booths or Tabernacles and then they began to mourn and weep (verse 9). Tabernacles was normally regarded as a time of rejoicing, so it seems strange that the people reacted in this way, especially as they had just observed the Day of Atonement when they would have made amends for wrongdoing.

Responding to God's Word in this way is not unlike King Josiah's reaction on hearing God's Word read out (2 Chronicles 34:19). The high priest had just rediscovered the Book of the Law while spring-cleaning the temple. Do you ever lose your Bible?

It is interesting how often in Ezra and Nehemiah strong emotions are expressed: anger, sadness, hate and then joy.

The joy of the Lord is spoken of at a time of intense pressure. It was not some happy, clappy, praise meeting. The people had just stood for the best part of five or six hours! Warren W. Wiersbe, in his book on Nehemiah,[17] speaks of the move from conviction to cleansing and then on to celebration. This was the line taken by Nehemiah when he called on the gathering to move on to celebration: 'The joy of the Lord is your strength' (verse 10).

The word for 'joy' used here occurs only in three other places (1 Chronicles 16:27; Ezra 6:16; Nehemiah 12:43–44). The Hebrew word means 'to be jubilant' (especially if you have just succeeded), 'to rejoice', 'to be joyful' and seems to mean 'a spiritual joy' in particular. (See the note on Ezra 3:12–13).

So the implication here would appear to be that with God there is joy-giving strength. Without God there is misery leading to weakness and apathy.

The Greek word for 'joy' used by Paul in describing the fruit of the Spirit (Galatians 5:22), is also a joy based on experiences of God.

The apostle Paul in prison and on trial for his life, wrote in a similar vein – 'rejoice in the Lord always. I will say it again: rejoice!' (Philippians 4:4). In Liverpool, another tough place to be sometimes, there is a saying, 'You have to laugh otherwise you cry.'

I think that these are all attempts at expressing the same realization. When we make a positive response to depression, oppression and outright times of trial, we can discover not only relief from the temptation, but an incredible ability to draw strength from our joy in God: a joy which does not depend on everything going smoothly all the time. It is not a joy afterwards but during times of trial. The call is still the same: no matter how tough life is, don't be sad, remember the joy of the Lord is your strength.

Questions

1. Does your Christian life go up and down according to the way you feel? How do you deal with it?
2. What do you think is the difference between joy and happiness?

3. The church often grows significantly in times of persecution and hardship. Why?

Nehemiah 8:13–18

Outdoor pursuits

**God does offer security, but in himself,
not in the things of this world.**

During the Feast of Tabernacles the
people lived in temporary shelters as a
reminder that when the Lord delivered
them from slavery in Egypt they had to
rely totally on him. Coming out of Egypt was only the
beginning. Too much reliance on possessions for their security led to selfishness and spiritual apathy. The second captivity was a harsh reminder of what happens when God is
ignored. So the Feast of Tabernacles was a symbolic way of
setting aside the material comforts of life in order to come
into the presence of God.

It is also called the Feast of the Seventh Month (verse
14), or the Festival of Booths. The date is the day after the
Law was read (8:2), the second day of Tishri. The Feast of
Tabernacles should begin on the fifteenth day of the
month (Leviticus 23:33; Numbers 29:12).

For some reason, which is not immediately obvious, the
Day of Atonement (*Yom Kippur*) is not mentioned. Some
scholars think that Ezra changed the dates: either that he
celebrated Tabernacles from the third to the tenth day, or
that he moved the Day of Atonement from the tenth to the
twenty-fourth day (9:1). It is an interesting thought, but if
it were true then there was not enough time to celebrate an
eight-day feast. It is more likely that Yom Kippur was not

yet a fixed date in the Jewish calendar. Even in Zechariah's time the Day of Atonement is only mentioned by the month and not the date (Zechariah 7:5; 8:19).

Jesus talked of having no security in a house when someone asked to follow him (Matthew 8:20). Others made excuses because their security was in possessions rather than Jesus. Paul discovered the secret of a satisfied life by looking to God for his security. In prison, and on trial for his life, he wrote a letter to the church at Philippi. In it he spoke of joy (4:4), satisfaction (4:12), and the conviction that God would look after his people (4:19).

Israel had to come out of Egypt, and Paul called on Christians not to compromise their faith: '"Therefore come out from them and be separate," says the LORD. "Touch no unclean thing and I will receive you"' (2 Corinthians 6:17).

There are lots of ways in which we need to come out. We need to come out from the security of church buildings. We need to come out from self-centred lifestyles. Then we can come into the presence of God.

Questions

1. If you could have three things on a desert island, what would you take with you?
2. Is it right for Christians to have plenty of everything?
3. How important are church buildings to the Christian faith?

Biblical terms

The Book of the Law of Moses
There are generally four views of what this was: a collection of legal documents; the Deuteronomic laws; the Pentateuch (the first five books of the Bible); or the priestly code of laws.

The phrase the 'Law of Moses' is used in the New Testament to refer to the Pentateuch (Luke 2:22; 24:44; John 7:23; Acts 13:39; 15:5; 28:23; 1 Corinthians 9:9. So there is no reason whatsoever to suppose that Ezra could not have brought back the Pentateuch from Babylon.

The whole company that had returned from exile (verse 17)
This phrase reveals an assumption which has been made before (Ezra 4:1, 4). That is, that there were no practising Jews who had remained behind in Judah, only those who had returned.

Nehemiah 9:1–5

The great confession

There can be no forgiveness until we are willing to say sorry.

The people gathered later in the month for a time of public confession, when they fasted and wore sackcloth (verse 1). Curiously, sackcloth or clothes are not mentioned anywhere else in Ezra or Nehemiah. It is rather a puzzle because the practice was well-known in the Old Testament.

Sackcloth was made of hair and used for sieving or straining liquids. The hair used was normally goat's hair which was black. It was also made into sacks for keeping grain in. The harshness of the cloth next to the body made it an effective aid to mourning, suffering and repentance (for example, Esther 4:1; Job 16:15; Isaiah 3:24; 58:5).

Suffering as a form of penitence has been a common religious practice over the centuries. During the Middle Ages pilgrims going to Canterbury would wear sackcloth. Some even crawled there on their hands and knees to heighten the experience – and the pain!

We read in Nehemiah that the people also separated themselves from all foreigners (verse 2). There is no reference here to Ezra's call to separate (Ezra 10). Some have speculated as to why Nehemiah does not connect the two occasions. It is my belief that there is no need to do so.

The first situation, in Ezra, involved men and women specifically within a family structure. Nehemiah's concern in this passage is the intermixing with foreigners in a time of confession for the nation of Israel, within an act of worship.

Although Deuteronomy 16:14 encourages aliens, or foreigners, to enjoy the celebration, can they take part in a time of confession for the nation? Nehemiah appears to think not. It is likely that this event led into the reforms which are recorded in chapter 13 and is not a direct reference to Ezra.

Confession is still considered an important part of both public and private worship. After all, how can there be forgiveness if there is no confession of guilt? James calls for believers to confess their faults to one another (James 5:16) and in 1 John we are told that when we confess our faults, God is faithful to forgive (1 John 1:9).

Just because we are Christians does not mean we never have any problems, or that we never make any mistakes. When God gave us a new start through his son Jesus, he made us clean. But it is like having a bath; it does not mean that we will never have to wash again. There will be times when we have to wash the dirt off, say we are sorry and get right with God and the people around us. The old saying is right: confession is good for the soul.

Questions

1. Why do you think some people feel it is necessary to suffer in some way before they can be forgiven by God?
2. What causes us to be so condemning of other people, while refusing to admit it when we make mistakes?
3. Should the church say sorry on behalf of a nation (see 2 Chronicles 7:14)?

Nehemiah 9:6–31

Yesterday

It is good to remember the past, not with sentimentality, but to learn from it.

As part of their act of worship together the Levites lead the people in thanksgiving to God for all his goodness to them as a nation. They recall again their history as a nation and how God has been with them throughout. Their prayer of praise and thanksgiving divides into three themes:

▶ *The birth of the nation under God* and the reasons for the first captivity in Egypt (verses 7–18).

▶ *The wanderings in the wilderness* for forty years following the exodus from Egypt, and God's goodness, guidance and provision during that period (verses 19–23)

▶ *Israel's entry into the land* that God had promised them, reflecting on Israel's unfaithfulness in times of plenty (verse 23–31).

There are times when we do not feel as close to God as we once were. Often it is when things are not as they should be.

When Israel was in Babylon the people began to think about home in a very sentimental way, like a Welshman a long way from home on Saint David's Day (see Psalm 137)! They had not learned from the past that the reason they were in Babylon was because they had ignored God. Time after time he had sent his prophets to speak to them and they had rejected them; a point that Jesus made to his Jewish listeners when he told the parable of the tenants of the vineyard (Luke 20:9–16).

If we look back just to remember 'the good old days', it can prevent us from moving on to the place where God wants us to be. Lot's wife is a fine example of someone who looked back for the wrong reason and ended up going nowhere (Genesis 19:17–26). The only good reason for looking back is to remember the goodness of God in times of testing, and to learn from the mistakes we have made.

Going the wrong way and learning from it is discovery. Repeating the experience is pure stupidity.

Questions

1 How do you take time to remember the things God has done for you in the past?
2. When people look back do they remember the good or the bad experiences and why?
3. Do you think that the church has learned from the mistakes of the past? If not, why not?

Times and seasons

Sabbath (verse 14)
This is the first mention of the Sabbath in either Ezra or Nehemiah. It seems unusual that, as a religious leader

involved in reform, Ezra did not raise the issue of the Sabbath at all.

Nehemiah, however, raises the issue of the Sabbath in a number of verses between here and chapter 13 (10:31; 13:15–22).

The Hebrew word means 'to rest', 'cease' or 'desist' and is closely linked to the word meaning 'the seventh'. So the Sabbath derives its name from the creation when God rested on the seventh day – Saturday. So what is good for God is good for his people, and keeping the Sabbath becomes a law (Exodus 20:8–11).

While the Jews operated a six-day working week, the Babylonians used a five-day system, although they did not adhere to it as strictly as the Jews. Once this holy day concept became law many Jewish scholars began to debate what could and could not be done on this day. For instance, it was forbidden to drag a chair because it was seen to create a furrow on an earth floor. So the person who did it would be guilty of ploughing.

Carrying loads or trading on the day of rest were Nehemiah's primary focus. Jesus observed the Sabbath (Luke 4:16) but his understanding of its purpose did differ from some of the religious leaders of his day (Matthew 12:1–14; Mark 2:23–28; Luke 6:1–11).

Christians later changed the day of rest from Saturday to Sunday and called it 'the Lord's day' (Revelation 1:10). They did this in remembrance of the fact that Jesus rose from the dead on a Sunday. This change in day led to some contention in the early days of the church (Romans 14:5).

Personalities

Abram (verse 7)

Abraham was first called Abram. To read about the circumstances surrounding the change in his name see Genesis 17:5.

Nehemiah 9:32–38

Today

God is not just a God of history, he is still present, powerful and dependable.

 This section begins with a reminder, in the image of a marriage, that God is faithful to his covenant. The problem is not God but his people; they are the ones who are lacking in loyalty.

The phrase 'a binding agreement' (verse 38) underlines this. Sometimes translated 'covenant', the word occurs only here and in Nehemiah 11:23. It means 'faithful support' or 'agreement', and comes from a root word meaning 'to confirm' or 'support', normally translated 'to believe', 'to endure', or 'to be faithful'. It is the word used of Abram (verse 8). In a number of translations verse 38 has been placed in chapter 10 as the first verse.

What is amazing is that God is still forgiving and faithful to his promises despite the failure, foolishness and weakness of his people. The point is made very clearly in the book of Hosea. There God's relationship with Israel is compared with that of Hosea and Gomer. The overall theme is that the love of God is as real, meaningful and forgiving today as it was yesterday.

Questions

1. How many times do you think you could forgive someone who has broken promises they made to you?
2. Why does God keep on loving us despite the way we sometimes treat him?

3. Is there anyone who you feel you will never be able to forgive?

Personnel

Slaves (verse 36)
In Jewish law Jews could serve as slaves for only six years, then they had to be set free (Exodus 21:2–11), unless they chose to remain in a state of slavery.

Jews who became slaves in Israel usually did so because of poverty in the family. A slave was worth around thirty shekels (Exodus 21:32) at a time when the average wage was around ten shekels a year. So this verse has in it the implication that the people are suffering a spiritual poverty because of disobedience. 'We are slaves today' (verse 36) 'because of our sins' (verse 37).

Nehemiah 10:1–29

For ever

The promise to be faithful to God is a promise which should last, like his love, for ever.

The reason the various leaders, officials, Levites and priests were gathered together and named was in order to carry out an oath of allegiance to God. It was very much a public act, naming names in order to ensure people kept their promises. Many of those mentioned are family names (15 of the 21 priestly names are family names and the leaders are mentioned almost completely by their family names). So what was promised was not just by individuals for themselves, but on behalf of complete families.

It is much more difficult to go back on your word in front of witnesses. You can be sure that if you do forget, there will always be someone to remind you.

The contract is with all those who have 'separated themselves' (verse 28). The words used here are associated with divorce on the one hand, and holiness on the other. The call to separate themselves from other nations is a call echoing Ezra (see the note on Ezra 10:11) to racial purity. But it was more than that, it was also a call away from idolatry. Idolatry often went hand in hand with mixing, especially through marriage, with other nations (for example 2 Kings 11:1–6). The word 'separate' implies the breaking off of a friendship. The promise was to put God and his temple first and to have no other gods, just like the marriage promise 'to forsake all others'.

That is what holiness is, to be set apart for God's purposes or 'elected'. The Jews sometimes mistook that calling to be set apart as a calling to be superior, when in fact it was a call to service. (See the note on Ezra 8:28.)

Some scholars have suggested that this group included those from other nations who had converted to Judaism, but the context makes it unlikely.[18]

The marriage act is used frequently as an image of the covenant that God's people have with him. Jesus also uses the image of the church as his bride. The marriage ceremony is always a public act, promises are made in front of witnesses, names are named. It is intended to encourage people to keep their promises as well as allowing a man and a woman to make a covenant with each other.

The Christian is called upon to do the same: Paul says, 'That if you confess with your mouth, "Jesus is Lord", and believe in your heart that God raised him from the dead, you will be saved' (Romans 10:9). It is like marriage except that it is not 'until death us do part', but for ever!

Questions

1. Does God ever break his promises to us?
2. Does the church ever break its promises to him?
3. Can you think of times when you have made your stand publicly for Jesus? Why did you do it?

Nehemiah 10:30–40

A contract with God

Putting God first in all things is not just an ideal, it is an imperative.

'The house of our God' is a phrase which is used nine times in this passage. Neglect of the temple was neglect of the covenant contract God had established with his people through Moses: a contract which is highlighted in the Decalogue (the Ten Commandments, Exodus 20:2–17).

The nation had been called to submit themselves to a covenant with God. Then they were called upon to separate themselves from the surrounding nations in order to be used by God. Now the call is to support the work of God as they had promised to do. All of this required them to keep their contract with God.

In the section on Nehemiah 9:14 we look at the Jewish concept of Sabbath. The seventh year, mentioned in verse 31, is a development of the same principle. It is a sabbatical year when even the land is given a rest: the 'fallow year' law (Exodus 23:10–11; Leviticus 25:1–7).

The seventh year was also the year when debts were

cancelled (Deuteronomy 15:1–18) and it was the time when Hebrew slaves were set free (Exodus 21:2–11; Jeremiah 34:14). This 'seventh-year' principle was intended to ensure justice for all in terms of social as well as religious values. Sadly it was not really observed (Jeremiah 34:8–16) because it affected people's pockets. Whenever cost is involved there seems to be compromise (Nehemiah 5:6–13).

Giving was obviously a key concern of Nehemiah and so the tithe, or giving of a tenth, is raised (verses 37–38). He reminds the people of their responsibility to give God the first-fruits, not the last (verses 35–37), a law which had not been observed for some time.

Following on from the theme of giving, the people are called to tithe (Nehemiah 12:44; 13:5). The failure to give to God is perceived as the cause of the crop failure as well as spiritual decline (Malachi 3:10).

The people still had to pay other taxes to the Persian ruler (Nehemiah 5:4) and before that to their own kings (1 Samuel 8:15, 17).

There is some debate about the New Testament's teaching on tithing, for there is no specific command to Christians to do so. The main references to tithing (Matthew 23:23; Luke 11:42; 18:12) involve condemnation of the religious and self-righteous. The other passage to mention tithing is Hebrews 7:2–9. There it is to do with paying the priest Melchizedek.

The only other clear indicator of giving in the church comes from Paul (2 Corinthians 8 and 9). He appears to set no limit on giving and appeals to generosity of heart: 'God loves a cheerful giver' (2 Corinthians 9:7).

We live in a society today where it seems everyone is concerned with their rights. The difficulty is that there is not the same enthusiasm for our responsibilities. That was Haggai's criticism – God's people were making sure they were comfortable but they neglected his house, the temple (Haggai 1:3).

It is true that today there are too many neglected church buildings. However, that is not what Paul is speaking about when he echoes the cry of Haggai about the temple. The temple of God (his house), under the new covenant in Christ, is Christian believers. Paul was calling the Christians at Corinth to face up to their responsibilities: 'Don't you know that you yourselves are God's temple and that God's Spirit lives in you? If anyone destroys God's temple, God will destroy him; for God's temple is sacred, and you are that temple' (1 Corinthians 3:16).

The way to make sure we don't neglect God's house (us) is to keep our contract with him. Jesus said, 'If you love me, you will obey what I command' (John 14:15). It is just like the marriage contract – love, honour and obey.

Someone once said that if you want real *joy* then you must put Jesus first, *o*thers second, and *y*ourself last. That is our contract with God.

Questions

1. Which is the easiest to remember, what I owe someone else, or how much they owe me?
2. Why is finance often a problem for the church?
3. Are there opportunities for Christians to take up their responsibilities to God in practical ways in your community, and if so how?

Faith in the city

Nehemiah 11:1 – 13:31

Nehemiah 11:1–19

Faith in the city

The nation could never be strong while the city was weak. There must be faith in the city in order to have faith in the nation.

The temple was rebuilt, the walls of the city were restored and there was a revival of the covenant between God and his people. There was even good news for the poor. Things were looking good, but there was just one problem: people just weren't queuing up to live in the city.

There were priests and Levites, as well as temple staff, living in Jerusalem. Some of the leaders involved in the administration also lived there, but it was not a balanced community – socially and economically.

We see a new perspective on tithing here, for the people sought the will of God for one in ten from every pure Jewish family to move back into the city. It was fine rebuilding Jerusalem, but not much would be achieved unless the people of God were prepared to have enough faith in their city to live there.

If it was taken over by Samaritans, Gentiles and the like, then who would be to blame when once again the temple and the walls fell into disrepair. Whose fault would it be when Jerusalem was not the 'Holy City of God'?

God could not find ten righteous people in the city of Sodom, and gave this as his reason for destroying it (Genesis 18:32). Ezekiel gives us a further insight into the destruction of Sodom when he states that it was destroyed because its people did not care for the poor and needy (Ezekiel 16:49).

Too often great cities have fallen into decay because the people of God have moved out to the comfortable suburbs. City churches have fallen into disrepair or been sold off to become temples of other faiths or made into warehouses and so on. Cities of the world have become the focus for all kinds of problems: poverty, crime, drugs, homelessness and godlessness; rarely have they become the focus of the glory of God.

The call of Nehemiah is still valid; to have faith in the city is to do something about it. Where are the one in ten Christians today who are prepared to sell up and move back into the cities in order to restore the faith of the nation? If we don't take our cities for God today, there is no hope for the rest of the nation tomorrow!

Questions

1. How many of us live within walking distance of the place where we worship?
2. Are there enough Christians living close to each other in your community to make a difference?
3. What does it mean for the people of God to be salt and light in the nation (see Matthew 5:13–16)?

Personnel

The leaders of the people (verse 1)
Nehemiah 7:4–5 hints that because of the small population of the city some of the nobles were encouraged to move in. This verse appears to confirm that this was true. In chapter 7 Nehemiah took the initiative; here it appears to be the people themselves that do so, so things were improving.

It is unlikely that this meant all the leaders. It was probably those who were most involved in the decision-making processes of the nation on both the religious and secular levels. Jerusalem would be the administrative centre for the province under Persian rule as well as the focal point of worship because of the temple.

Nehemiah 11:20–36

Town and country

It is important to recognize God's presence wherever we live, not just in special places, and also to be aware of our part in his plans.

Thirty-two towns, villages or farms are listed here as being at least partly occupied by Jewish people, in an area which was traditionally allocated to the tribes of Judah and Benjamin.

It would be perfectly natural for people returning from exile to want to return to their home towns, back to their roots where they felt they belonged. Belonging, however, has to be in the perspective of the wider community of the people of God: not just 'you in your small corner and I in mine'.

This passage not only names the towns, but also locates them in the country. Each has its part to play and, therefore, is worthy of mention.

I feel certain that it was Nehemiah's concern that every devout Jew should feel involved in the restoration of Jerusalem. So it would be with this in mind that he looked to 'the rest of the people' (Nehemiah 11:1) to send members of their families to live in Jerusalem.

Pethaniah (verse 24) has another part to play in God's plans. He was the king's agent for the region and you can be sure that, as a practising Jew, he was also working for *the* King!

It is a firm reminder that God has a part for each one of us to play, no matter how insignificant we may feel we are. It is important to know how God wants to use us where we live, but also to understand that we also belong to the worldwide family of God's people through our blood-ties in Jesus Christ.

The great challenge is to be 'salt and light', an influence for good (Matthew 5:13–16), wherever we are, and to proclaim the good news of Jesus: the opportunity for forgiveness and a new beginning for all who want to be a part of his family.

Paul, the apostle, puts it clearly when he writes, 'in Christ we who are many form one body, and each member belongs to all the others' (Romans 12:5).

Sometimes we can feel isolated, but we are not. As Christians we are all part of God's mighty army. When you feel you are struggling, remember these words by Ishmael, a Christian songwriter and singer: 'we may be weak as soldiers – but as an army we are strong'.[19]

Questions

1. How does my church relate to the worldwide church of Jesus Christ?
2. What did Jesus mean when he prayed, 'that all of them may be one, Father, just as you are in me and I am in you' (John 17:21)?
3. How can I be the King's agent where I live?

Nehemiah 12:1–26

God's worship leaders

The chief purpose of man (including woman) is to glorify God.

It was always the priestly families who would lead the people of God into his presence in public worship. There are twenty-two names listed here. They are  names which have caused some discussion amongst scholars. Twenty-four people were normally required to fulfil the temple duties (1 Chronicles 24:1–18), so some have suggested that this list is a faulty copy which has resulted in two names being dropped. Another possibility is that these were still early days in the restoration of Jerusalem and therefore everything was not yet fully operational.

The first list of families is identified by its family heads, those who had returned from exile in Babylon with Zerubbabel and Jeshua in 537BC, just after King Cyrus' proclamation.

The second list is of the Levitical families at the time of the return from exile. Ezra 2:40 only mentions Jeshua and Kadmiel as leaders of the seventy-four Levites who came home, and the family name Hodaviah. The Levites were given the responsibility for leading thanksgiving and praise in the great celebration (verses 8, 24). They were also gatekeepers and guardians of the store-rooms of the temple.

The list we have here seems to be a slightly contracted version and we can fill in a little more detail by referring to Ezra 3:9 and Nehemiah 3:24.

The third list concerns the priests of Joiakim's time

(verses 12–21). This list, like the others, confirms that the priestly families retained their ancestral names and did not change them every time a new leader was appointed. In this register of names the Hattush family is left out (12:12) and other names appear to be given different spellings.

If, as some have suggested, this is a later addition, it seems strange that the editor would include the same names in the same passage with different spellings. However, a more probable explanation is that the family names were kept but over time the spelling changed. This would also do more to confirm the authenticity of the list.

It has been quite common in recent times for Jews moving from one country to another to modify their names in order to adapt to the new culture – Levi, Levine, Levinski.

The final list is the heads of the Levites in Eliashib's time (verses 22–26). The date would have been around 450BC and onwards. Time was usually measured in terms of the lifespans of the high priests before there were kings in Israel. It appears that with the demise of the rule of kings, time was again measured in relation to priests and Levites.

The New Testament develops the concept of priesthood. It puts the emphasis on Jesus as the great high priest (Hebrews 4:14–16), and Peter describes those who are disciples of Jesus as 'a royal priesthood, a holy nation' (1 Peter 2:5). Out of interest, the Latin word for priest means 'bridge-maker'.

Today each one who answers the call to follow Jesus joins the priesthood of all believers. Everyone who believes has a responsibility to come before God regularly in worship, thanksgiving and praise. No longer is it valid to believe there is some form of priesthood to carry out these responsibilities on our behalf: it is my duty and should be my delight. We live in a world where everyone seems to be concerned with their *rights*; but this is our *responsibility*. This is the new covenant.

Questions

1. Do you worship only when you feel like it? If so, do you pay your taxes on the same basis?
2. Is Jesus the only go-between (bridge) necessary between you and the heavenly Father?
3. What do you think the role of the priest is, as mentioned in 1 Peter 2:5?

Personalities

And Joiarib (verses 6, 19)
Joiarib was an ancestor of the famous Jewish freedom-fighting family, the Maccabees, in the time of the Greek empire (1 Maccabees 2:1 in the Apocrypha). The name also appears in the list in 1 Chronicles 24 as one of the priestly divisions. The NIV misses out the 'and' before Joiarib's name, but it is there in the Hebrew. It was probably meant to indicate that the names which followed were taken from a second list.[20]

Sherebiah (verse 8): this name is also found in Nehemiah 8:7; 9:4 and 10:12.

Mattaniah (verse 8) and *Bakbukiah* (verse 9) also occur in Nehemiah 11:17 and 12:25.

Unni (verse 9) is a variation on the name Ananiah or Anaiah (compare 1 Chronicles 15:18, 20 with Nehemiah 8:4 and 3:23).

The family names are also found in the list of King David's musicians in 1 Chronicles 25:4, with the same responsibilities.

Families of the high priests are next (verses 10–11). 1 Chronicles 6:3–15 gives the lineage of the high priests from Aaron to Jehozadak. Jehozadak was high priest at the time of the exile (Ezra 3:8; 5:2; 10:18; Haggai 1:1; Zechariah 6:11).

Jeshua (verse 10) was Unni's son (Ezra 3:2) and was one of those who returned in 538BC.

Joiakim (verse 10) was high priest in the period between the return of Jeshua and Zerubbabel and the return of Nehemiah.

Eliashib (verse 10) was high priest during Nehemiah's governorship (Nehemiah 3:1, 20–21; 13:28).

Joiada (verse 10) was related to Sanballat (Nehemiah 13:28).

Jonathan (verse 11) is sometimes thought to be the same person as Johanan because the historian Josephus[21] names him as the next high priest after Eliashib. This is not my view, especially as Josephus is notorious for getting both his facts and dates confused.

Jaddua (verse 11) according to Josephus[22] is high priest at the time of Alexander the Great which would be about 332BC. If he is correct, then Jaddua must have been about a hundred years of age by then. It is more reasonable to assume that this was a family name and therefore there was more than one Jaddua who was high priest over the years.

Ezra (verse 13) is an alternative form of Azaniah (see the note on Ezra 7:1).

Zechariah (verse 16) is the prophet of the book of that name. He is a descendant of Iddo. In his book he calls the nation to restore moral standards.

Jedaiah (verse 19 and verse 20) is a name which appears twice and would seem to confirm the idea that they were actually two different people.

Darius the Persian (verse 22): The question is, which Darius? Was it Darius the Great (522–486BC), Darius II, also called Nothus (423–405BC), or Darius III also known as Codomannus (335–330BC) and last ruler of the Persian Empire before the conquest of Alexander the Great?

The date which best fits the context is Darius II and this is supported by the *Elephantine Papyri* which record that Johanan, Bagoli and Sanballat all held office during the reign of Darius II.[23]

Nehemiah 12:27–30

Come on and celebrate!

Although the work was done by human hands, it was God who made it possible. He should be given his rightful place – it is his party.

This passage takes us back into Nehemiah's diary for an account of what happened next: the dedication of the wall. It was not only temples which were singled out for celebrations. The completion of the wall was Nehemiah's greatest achievement and the climax of his governorship.

Worship leaders were brought in from the surrounding towns and villages including singers, choirs and musicians. This was going to be some celebration!

As with any great celebration there was plenty of planning to do if it was going to be done properly. Levites were sent to the Jewish communities surrounding Jerusalem. It was going to be a holy day and a holiday, so everyone and everything involved had to be purified. After all, this celebration was in God's honour. This was to be a time of thanksgiving to him as well as the dedication of all that had been achieved in his name.

Not many people would dream of inviting the Queen of Britain to a party without spending a good deal of time in planning and preparation. Most people would take a lot of time and trouble to ensure the place was clean and tidy. Personal appearance would be a priority as well. They would want everything to look its best and the aim would be to make a good impression with their 'VIP' visitor. If given the chance, they would almost certainly want to invite all their family, friends and neighbours.

Is that how we prepare for worship – the time when we come in a very special way into the presence of the King of kings?

Isaiah did not feel right in the presence of a holy God until he was clean right through (Isaiah 6:6–8), then his heart's desire was to serve God in the very best way possible.

When the woman at the well met Jesus, she simply had to invite everyone she knew to come and meet him (John 4:29). As a result many of them became believers and wanted Jesus to stay with them (John 4:39–40).

The pattern that Nehemiah followed in preparing for worship was this: preparation, purification and praise. His invitation was, 'come on and celebrate'.

Questions

1. How do you prepare for coming into the presence of God in worship?
2. Is your experience of him so exciting that you want to invite everyone you know to come and join in thanksgiving with you?
3. Would your church dedicate a wall, a car or a fridge if they believed God had provided it for them?

Temple worship

Harps and lyres (verse 27)

Sometimes translated 'harps and zithers', these were stringed instruments and were made of cypress wood. The first was plucked with the fingers, and the second was strummed with a plectrum. The lyre was the first instrument to be mentioned in the Bible (Genesis 4:21); it had about ten strings on it, as did the harp.

Biblical terms

Purified (verse 30)

Before any time of significant worship there was always some form of ritual purification (compare Ezra 6:20). The exact form which the purification took is not mentioned, but various laws and traditions allow us to make an educated guess.

For those ministering at the dedication, purification would almost certainly mean fasting, ritual washing and abstaining from sexual intercourse.

There were very clear links between ritual purification and dedication or consecration to God. Impurity could occur as a result of food eaten, the touching of various forms of dead flesh, childbirth, skin infections, mildew on clothing, bodily discharges, unlawful sexual relationships, and even lawful ones at the wrong time! (For more details see Leviticus 11–19.) Any state of impurity would separate the believer from God.

Jesus takes this a stage further when he states that wrong relationships between believers will have the same effect (Matthew 5:23–24).

Nehemiah 12:31-43

Feet were made for walking

A walk of witness, worship and praise lets everyone know of the presence and provision of God.

 The procession of praise has something of the flavour of Joshua and the Israelites when they marched around the city of Jericho, but Joshua was outside the city – these people were on the walls!

The walls had been worked on and watched over. Now the people were worshipping God while standing on them.

The procession was in two parts, one setting off to the right, and other to the left, in order to meet half-way round.

Apart from proclaiming the ability of the living God to help his people achieve the seemingly impossible task, Nehemiah was also making a point to his enemies. Remember how the opposition had sneered at the Jewish attempts to repair the walls, how they had said that even a fox was not safe walking on it (Nehemiah 4:3)?

Now there were two processions going around it, each being led by one of the two key people, under God, who had made it possible: Ezra and Nehemiah! Ezra took the south-bound group and Nehemiah the group heading north.

Each procession was led by a choir, followed by dignitaries in order of importance. There was enough room for people to walk three-abreast along it.[24] It started from the Valley Gate (see the note on Nehemiah 2:13, 15) with the two groups eventually joining up again at the temple. The sacrifices that were made then followed the same pattern as when the altar and the temple were dedicated (Ezra 3:3–5; 6:17).

The atmosphere was one of worship as not only the religious leaders but many families participated. As on each of the significant moments previously recorded in Ezra and Nehemiah, it was a cause for great joy: a joy so powerful that the noise of it was heard far away!

God had brought his people back to their land, the temple had been rebuilt, and now Jerusalem had been restored. Something exciting had been happening to the people through these events. They too had experienced restoration. God's people had rediscovered deliverance, determination and dedication in their efforts to restore the glory of Almighty God in the land.

Whenever there has been any significant movement of the Spirit of God there have been processions of his people proclaiming his glory.

In recent times Christians have initiated something called 'March for Jesus'. A relatively small number of people in London, England, wanted to proclaim the name of Jesus in their city, so they had a march through the city centre. Since then the movement has grown. There have been marches across every major town and city in Britain, many of the cities of Europe and throughout the world.

The pattern has been similar to that of Nehemiah: processions led by worship groups; witnessing to the power and provision of God in their lives; demonstrating the power of the Almighty to overcome the opposition; and not forgetting a real sense of joy. The impact has been felt far and wide.

Public proclamation of the saving power of Jesus, sharing not only his love but also his joy, is one of the essential ingredients of a living church, a church that is on the march.

Two New Testament quotes come to mind: 'Go into all the world and preach the good news to all creation' (Mark 16:15) and, 'with your feet fitted with the readiness that comes from the gospel of peace' (Ephesians 6:15). Feet were made for walking.

Questions

1. Has God done something in your life that you want to shout about? If so, what?
2. Why do you think that Christians often appear to prefer staying in when Jesus said, 'Go out?'
3. What do you think the other people of Nehemiah's time thought of his walk of witness?

Personnel

Two large choirs (verse 31)
The Hebrew word which the NIV translates as 'choir' actually means 'giving thanks' or 'thanksgiving'. If you spoke to someone in Hebrew today you would use this word to say 'thank you'. So a choir is a group of people gathered together to give thanks.

There were two choirs: a southern and a northern one.

The southbound choir (verses 31–37) is listed first. It has seven priests (verses 33–35) and the choirmaster is Zechariah (verse 35). There are eight musicians (verse 36) and the rest of the group comprises half the leaders of Judah (verse 32) including Ezra (verse 36).

The northbound choir (verses 38–43) is similar in composition. There are seven priests (verse 41). Jezrahiah is the choirmaster (verse 42) and it also has eight musicians (verse 42). Nehemiah is in this procession (verse 38) as well as the other half of the officials (verse 40). What the choir sang is not recorded but scholars have linked Psalm 147 with this occasion.[25]

175

Biblical terms

Could be heard far away (verse 43)
In Ezra 3:13 the noise the people made at the foundation-laying ceremony could also be heard far away. The one big difference is that then it was hard to distinguish between the weeping and shouts of joy; there was no such difficulty here!

Nehemiah 12:44–47

Maintaining ministry

The labourer deserves to be rewarded for work done.

Part of the promise the people of God had made was to pay their share in maintaining the temple and ministry (Nehemiah 10). The priests, Levites, temple gatekeepers and musicians all needed to live, so Nehemiah ensured that they were not taken for granted. He encouraged the people to give, but the Levites had the responsibility of 'taking the plate round'.

They went out to the surrounding towns and villages to take up collections to maintain the ministry of the temple; it was not a freewill offering but an obligatory collection. The spirituality of Israel was at a high point at this time so the people gave gladly.

Something of the same feel existed in the New Testament church. After Pentecost, when people were being added daily to the church, there were few money problems. They willingly shared what they had with those in need (Acts 4:32), with one or two notable exceptions (Acts 5:1–11).

Even when the church in Jerusalem experienced a time of famine Paul could write to other churches around the Roman Empire encouraging them to give. He encouraged them with the words, 'God loves a cheerful giver' (2 Corinthians 9:7) and challenged the churches to out-give each other.

When people are blessed by God through his servants, it is only natural (supernatural) to want to give to God and his work. Giving should be not just a duty, but a delight.

There are three kinds of giving: grudge-giving, nudge-giving and thanks-giving. The only one the Almighty really finds acceptable is thanksgiving.

Questions

1. Could I survive if God gave me nine times as much as I give him and I had to live on it?
2. Do you think people of God should be paid, or should they earn their own keep?
3. Why do so many churches in Britain seem to have difficulties raising money for the upkeep of the buildings, and maintenance of ministry?

Biblical terms

First-fruits (verse 44)

Better translated 'the prime fruits' because the offering given to God was not necessarily the first to ripen but the best. The word 'first' comes from a Hebrew root word meaning 'prime', 'chief' or 'head', indicating the very best of its kind.

The same word is used in 10:37, but 13:31 uses a different word meaning 'the first fruit to ripen'.

Geography

From the fields around the towns (verse 44)
The size of each town's contribution to the temple was
assessed according to the amount of farmland it included.

Nehemiah 13:1–3

Keep it clean!

**God's people are called to be in
the world but not of it.**

Nehemiah kept his promise to the Persian king, Artaxerxes, and returned to the
palace after the task of restoring the wall
(and the people) had been completed.
There is an old saying, 'while the cat is away the mice
will play', and that seemed to be exactly the situation in
Judah after Nehemiah's return to Babylon. Now it was
necessary, all over again, for the Jews to 'clean up their act'
and separate themselves from the foreigners in the land.
Those listed in the category 'All who were of foreign
descent' (verse 3) included not only Ammonites and
Moabites, but any Jew who had non-Jewish ancestors, that
is, was of mixed blood. We know that this restriction was
not put into action fully, otherwise all of King David's
descendants would have been excluded: his grandmother,
Ruth, was a Moabite (Ruth 1:4; compare Matthew 1:5). My
feeling is that it means immigrants who have no Jewish

blood, rather than the other way round. As in 9:2, there is no reference to separating from foreign wives, but the Jews were told to clean up their act.

The early church used a ship as a symbol for the church. It is a good way of understanding the nature and mission of the covenant people of God. We are called to weather out the storms of life, sailing wherever the wind of the Spirit takes us and with Jesus Christ as our anchor. A ship on the sea is safe as long as the water is outside the ship and not inside. Christians are safe while they remember to be in the world but not of the world.

Someone once made the observation, 'the church is called to be in the world, but we must not allow the world to infect the church'. Our commitment is to do things God's way without compromise, and not allow the pressure of the people to get in the way.

The trend of the world, as seen in the story of Baalam, is to do what the majority want and think: to go along with the crowd or risk persecution. But the outcome is still the same: God blesses those who are persecuted for his sake (Matthew 5:11–12).

The call to the church today is the same call given in the time of Nehemiah, Keep it clean!

Questions

1. What sort of pressures are there on Christians today to compromise their faith?
2. What would you say to someone who told you that Christians should not be so arrogant in insisting that Jesus Christ is the only way to heaven?
3. What is your church's view of what God says in his Word about homosexuality, abortion and war?

Biblical terms

Ammonite or Moabite (verse 1)
Both were Lot's descendants from his incestuous encounter
with his daughters (Genesis 19:33–38), which is probably
why they are linked together as unacceptable relationships,
despite the fact that the encounter with Balaam only
involved the Moabites (Numbers 22 – 25).

Personalities

Balaam (verse 2)
Balaam was a pagan seer and sorcerer who was hired by
the king of Moab to curse Israel, but his curses were
turned into blessings (Numbers 23:11; 24:1, 10).

Nehemiah 13:4–9

Cleansing the temple

Making room for God means getting rid of the rubbish.

Nehemiah obtained permission from
Artaxerxes to pay a return visit to
Jerusalem (verse 6) and as he does so
the account returns to the first person,
indicating that he is again drawing on his diary.

How easily the people had settled down to a comfortable compromise after Nehemiah's departure. His arch-enemy Tobiah (an Ammonite!) had taken up lodgings in the temple (verses 4–5). The fact that he had married into one of the priestly families, and his son into another, helped him to move in. Many of the Jewish leaders had made an oath of allegiance to him. This kind of oath implies clan loyalties through blood ties and/or a political affiliation. (See the section on Ezra 10:5.) 'A room in the courts' (verse 7) would be a room of some size opening up into the courtyard of the temple. The word which is trans-lated 'a room' suggests not only a store-room but also living accommodation (1 Chronicles 9:26; 2 Chronicles 31:11; Ezra 8:29; Nehemiah 10:38–40).

The presence of a non-Jew here would require purifica-tion of the whole area from ritual uncleanness. (See the note on Nehemiah 12:30).

On his return, Nehemiah had no hesitation: he threw Tobiah out with all his belongings. Then he set about having the temple rooms purified. What must have really annoyed him was the fact that Tobiah had taken over rooms set aside for the offerings for the temple staff and the incense for God.

This event links with the time when Jesus entered the temple and threw out the money-changers, accusing them of making his father's house a den of robbers instead of a house of prayer (Matthew 21:13; Mark 11:17; Luke 19:46; he was quoting from Isaiah 56:7 and Jeremiah 7:11).

It is so easy for things to creep into the life of the church through wrong relationships and unholy alliances. Once things, or people, which are nothing to do with God move into the body of Christ, it does not take long for the rot to set in. As mentioned, it is like the bad apple – it takes only one to gradually affect and infect all the rest.

The only way to put things right is to 'take the bull by the horns', and get rid of them completely. Holiness is not negotiable; cleanse the temple!

Questions

1. What connection is there between a jolly fat man with reindeer and the birth of Jesus?
2. Does your church think it is acceptable to God to hold an act of worship with people of other faiths, each praying to their own deity?
3. Can you think of examples of people or things which have moved in and taken over the place of God in your life?

Times and seasons

Thirty-second year of Artaxerxes (verse 6)
That is, 433BC, but we do not know the exact date of Nehemiah's return visit. Inasmuch as he came with Artaxerxes' permission it has to be before the king's death in 423BC.

Personalities

Eliashib (verse 4)
This was not Eliashib the high priest of 3:1, 20–21; 12:10, 22, and 13:28. This Eliashib is not referred to as high priest; his responsibility was to look after the temple rooms, the equivalent of a dean. He certainly would gain from letting out the rooms. The fact that Eliashib the high priest was related to Sanballat, another of Nehemiah's foes (13:28) probably helped.

A similar incident happened in Egypt when King Cambyses cleansed the temple of the god Neith, having thrown out foreigners.[26]

Nehemiah 13:10-14

Robbing God

Neglecting the things of God will always lead to problems.

What a change from 12:44-47 when the people were so willing to give. Now they have moved from thanks-giving to grudge-giving. The financial crisis at the temple was so great that many of the temple staff had been forced to go home in order to have enough to eat (verse 11).

It was necessary for Nehemiah to put God's house in order. He was not a priest, but it looks as though the high priest was not doing his job properly because of self-interest. First he got the temple staff back and then set up a finance committee.

The people he chose were appointed not for their skills, but their trustworthiness. Too often people are appointed for their ability rather than their spirituality, but Nehemiah had played before!

Almost the last words of the Old Testament in the book of Malachi are on the same topic – robbing God. His plea was, 'Bring the whole tithe into the storehouse, that there may be food in my house' (Malachi 3:10). The promise which follows is that if the people will respond, God will bring them a blessing so great they will not be able to contain it (Malachi 3:11). Presumably they ignored the call because soon after Alexander the Great came, took over the land and desecrated the temple.

Not much has changed; there are still churches which struggle to survive financially because the members give God the left-overs instead of the best, while others have rediscovered that what Malachi said is really true and their churches grow.

Someone once said to me, 'You can never out-bless God, but it is great fun trying.' The message is plain, give to God and he will give to you; rob God and you will deprive yourself.

Questions

1. Which do you think comes first, financial problems or spiritual lethargy? Why?
2. If you were appointing a treasurer, musician or secretary for your church, what qualities would you look for?
3. Why do you think some Christians begrudge giving to God's work when he gave even his only son for us?

History

Portions assigned to Levites (verse 10)
These were the tithes mentioned in 10:37 which the people had promised to give. It may be that the Levites had not gone and collected them as was expected (12:44). It is also interesting that although technically Levites did not own land (Deuteronomy 14:29; 18:1; Numbers 18:20–24) other than grazing land around their towns, these did (verse 10). So the ownership of land may have led to a conflict of interests for the Levites.

Nehemiah 13:15–22

Rest versus riches

However busy and demanding life is, there should always be time for God and time for relaxation.

The first promise made is the hardest to break; after that it gets easier. Compromising with unbelievers, giving God the left-overs and putting riches before rest and reflection. One by one the Jews broke the promises they had made so enthusiastically some time before (Nehemiah 10:31).

The Law as given by Moses specifically stated that the Sabbath was to be a day of rest (Exodus 20:8–11), even the animals are given a break (Exodus 23:12). So making wine, loading grain and using donkeys was very much against the Law, let alone the covenant of chapter 10.

'My own men' (verse 19) suggests that Nehemiah did not trust the local inhabitants to keep the gates closed. 'Night by the wall' (verse 21) refers to a method employed by tradespeople hoping to get to the head of the queue for the start of business (rather as people nowadays queue up the night before the Harrods' sale begins). There was also the added possibility of doing some illegal trading with the guards or townspeople via baskets hung over the wall during the night.

Unbelievers put temptation in the way when they came to trade on the Sabbath. In fact, Nehemiah had to order the city gates to be closed just before the Sabbath began at sundown and not to be opened until the end of the Sabbath at sundown the following day.

How often throughout history the desire for power and wealth has overcome principles. It began in the garden of

Eden (Genesis 3:5), it prevented the rich young man from following Jesus (Matthew 19:16–24) and it caused the downfall of Ananias and Sapphira (Acts 5:1–10).

The church at the time of the Reformation was split because of a monk called Martin Luther. He took on the role of Nehemiah and challenged the church over their corruption and accumulation of wealth and failure to practise what they preached.

William Wilberforce had a struggle on his hands when he sought to abolish the slave-trade because many of the slave-owners were church-attending people who were not willing to sacrifice wealth for the sake of freedom for their slaves.

Lord Shaftesbury experienced similar problems when he fought for better working conditions in the factories and the mines. Too many mine and mill owners were church-going people who would lose money from the reforms.

Today Christians observe Sunday as a special day of rest, relaxation and reflection. The Jewish rest day, Saturday, changed to Sunday to remind believers that Jesus rose from the grave on Easter Sunday.

Wealth and power still get in the way of God's people. Changes to Sunday-trading law have meant even some Christian-based companies now operate on Sundays through fear of losing out financially if they stick to their principles. And people worry that they will lose their jobs if they don't work on Sundays. Some people have to work on Sundays, such as doctors, police and preachers, but it is the motivation that is in question. Is it necessary, or just financially beneficial?

God worked on creation for six days and rested on the seventh (Genesis 2:3). We are made in his image and called to live his way. Jesus summed it up when he said, 'You cannot serve both God and money' (Matthew 6:24; Luke 16:13).

Apparently the French agnostic, Voltaire, said, 'If you want to kill Christianity, you must abolish Sunday.' It is rest versus riches, and we have to choose.

Questions

1. Do you have a regular day off to relax and also spend time with God?
2. What would your church say if you had a normal Monday to Saturday job but your boss wanted you to work Sundays?
3. Imagine you live with your family but they are not Christians. You discover they are using electricity illegally. What would you do?

Nehemiah 13:23–31

Drawing the line

Non-believers usually cause their partners to move away from God.

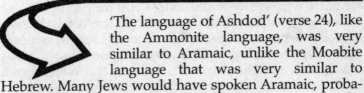

'The language of Ashdod' (verse 24), like the Ammonite language, was very similar to Aramaic, unlike the Moabite language that was very similar to Hebrew. Many Jews would have spoken Aramaic, probably a slightly different dialect, but Hebrew was and is the language of Jewish worship for the orthodox Jew.

Language is an important aspect of national identity. It was no different for the Jews then than it is for the Welsh today, for example.

On the surface the main issue is mixed marriages, but the underlying issue was the danger of losing national identity. This is why Nehemiah's complaint is that half the children of mixed marriages did not know how to speak the language of the Jews.

This would be a particularly sensitive problem with so many Jews living in other lands, and the dangers of assimilation (2 Kings 18:26, 28; 2 Chronicles 32:8; Isaiah 36:11).

So from Nehemiah's perspective it was about the survival of God's covenant people. There is sometimes a fine line between maintaining a national identity and carrying out racial cleansing of the kind that Adolf Hitler would impose on the Jews many years later.

The same kind of situation arose in the New Testament church when non-Jews at Antioch became followers of Jesus. Gentile believers were not willing to follow Jewish practices, but James ruled they could be part of the church. The dilemma was whether the Jewish Christians should give up their national identity by forsaking the basic principles of their way of life, such as kosher food laws and circumcision (Acts 15:1–29).

A similar issue arose out of Christians marrying non-Christians. Paul advised against it for the same reason as Nehemiah (2 Corinthians 6:14). Christians marrying non-believers today still run up against a number of problems. There will be conflicts of interest and probably beliefs. It is quite common for the unbelieving partner to pull the Christian away from faith and fellowship. When children are born, whose way and example will they follow?

The only way to avoid this sort of conflict is to stay away from partnerships that lead to this sort of temptation. Paul's comment on this subject is powerful, '...what fellowship can light have with darkness? ... What does a believer have in common with an unbeliever?' (2 Corinthians 6:14–15)

Put another way, can oil and water mix?

Questions

1. Is it easier to be a Christian when you are with other Christians or when you are with non-believers?
2. If someone in the family laughs at you because of your beliefs, how do you react?

3. If your non-Christian partner were to say to you 'If you really love me don't go to church', what would you say?

Biblical terms

Tore out their hair (verse 25)
Hair pulling was a common practice of Old Testament times. Isaiah 50:6 suggests that beard plucking was a form of punishment and 2 Samuel 10:4–5 suggests that a man who had forcibly had his beard removed was the subject of humiliation (see also the comments on Ezra 9:1–7).

Solomon's sin (verse 26)
Solomon made treaties with other nations in order to improve trade and maintain peace in the land. In order to achieve this he entered into a number of marriages with daughters of nobles of those lands. When they came to Jerusalem they brought images of their gods with them and the tension began (1 Kings 3:12; 11:1–6).

Personalities

Eliashib and Sanballat (verse 28)
Blood ties with the priesthood led to the same sort of difficulties for Eliashib (Leviticus 21:14 expressly forbids the high priest to marry a foreigner). So it should have come as no great surprise to him when Nehemiah threw out Joiada, his son. Especially as Sanballat was one of the main people to oppose Nehemiah in his efforts to rebuild the walls of Jerusalem (see the note on Nehemiah 2:10).

Notes

1 Winton Thomas, *Documents from Old Testament Times* (Harper and Row, 1961), pp. 84–86.

2 S. Baron, *A Social and Religious History of the Jews* (Columbia University Press, 1952), p. 162.

3 J. Finegan, *Handbook of Biblical Chronology* (Princeton University Press, 1964), pp. 212–213.

4 F. Vallat, 'L'Inscription Cuneiform Trilingue (D.Sab)', *Journal Asiatique* 260 (1972), p. 249.

5 *The Babylonian Talmud* (TB Sanhedrin 936).

6 Herodotus, *History* 3:34 (Everyman, 1992 edition), p. 233.

7 J. B. Pritchard (ed.), *Ancient Near Eastern Texts* (Princeton University Press, 1958), p. 492.

8 Ibid., p. 492.

9 Josephus, *Antiquities* 12:160–236, translated by William Whiston (Shapiro Valentine & Co., 1960), pp. 338–339.

10 Kathleen M. Kenyon, *Digging Up Jerusalem* (Book Club Associates, 1975), p. 185.

11 Ibid., p. 182.

12 F. M. Cross, 'Geshem the Arab, Enemy of Nehemiah', *Biblical Archaeologist* 18 (1955), pp. 46–47.

13 Josephus, *Antiquities* 11.5.8 translated by William Whiston (Shapiro Valentine & Co., 1960), p. 313.

14 N. Avigad, 'Bullae and Seals from a Post-exilic Judean Archive', *Quedeh: Monographs of the Institute of Archaeology* 4 (Jerusalem Hebrew University, 1976), pp. 1–20.

15 Kathleen M. Kenyon, *Digging Up Jerusalem* (Book Club Associates, 1975), p. 110.

16 Josephus, *Antiquities* 11:179, translated by William Whiston (Shapiro Valentine & Co., 1960), p. 314.

17 Warren W. Wiersbe, *Be Determined* (Scripture Press, 1992), p. 101.

18 D. J. Clines, *Ezra, Nehemiah, Esther* (Marshall, Morgan & Scott Ltd., 1984), p. 205.

19 'We are in God's Army', by Ian Smale (Thank You Music, 1987).

20 L. H. Brockington, *Ezra, Nehemiah and Esther* (NCB Nelson, 1969), p. 155.
21 Josephus, *Antiquities* 11.7.1, translated by William Whiston (Shapiro Valentine & Co., 1960), p. 322.
22 Ibid., 11.8.4, p. 324.
23 F. M. Cross, 'The Discovery of the Samaria Papyri', *The Biblical Archaeologist* 26 (1963), pp. 110–121; F. M. Cross, 'Aspects of Samaritan and Jewish History in Late Persian and Hellenistic Times', *Harvard Review* 59, (1966), pp. 201–211.
24 Kathleen M. Kenyon, *Jerusalem* (Thames and Hudson, 1967), p. 115.
25 L. H. Brockington, *Ezra, Nehemiah and Ezra* (NCB Nelson, 1969), p. 160.
26 Edwin M. Yamauchi, *Persia and the Bible* (Baker Book House, 1990), p. 106.

For further reading

P. R. Ackroyd, *Chronicles, Ezra, Nehemiah* (London: SCM, 1973)

Joseph Blenkinsop, *Ezra-Nehemiah* (London: SCM, 1989)

L. H. Brockington, *Ezra, Nehemiah and Esther* (London: NCB Nelson, 1969)

D. J. A. Clines, *Ezra, Nehemiah, Esther* (London: Marshall Morgan and Scott, 1984)

F. Charles Fensham, *The Books of Ezra, Nehemiah and Esther* (Grand Rapids: Eermans, 1991)

Derek Kidner, *Ezra and Nehemiah* (Leicester: IVP, 1979)

J. Carl Laney, *Ezra-Nehemiah* (Chicago: Moody Press, 1982)

Warren W. Wiersbe, *Be Determined* (Amersham on the Hill: Scripture Press, 1992)

H. G. M. Williamson, *Ezra, Nehemiah* (Waco Texas: Word Books, 1985)

Edwin Yamauchi, *Ezra, Nehemiah* (Grand Rapids: Regency Reference Library Zondervan, 1988)

Edwin Yamauchi, *Persia and the Bible* (Grand Rapids: Baker Book House, 1990)